HEAVEN WITHIN

Restoring Wholeness
For Better Leadership

CANDACE MAE

ONYX PUBLISHING

First published in 2022 by Onyx Publishing, an imprint of Notebook Publishing of Notebook Group Limited, 20–22 Wenlock Road, London, N1 7GU.

www.onyxpublishing.com

ISBN: 9781913206420

A CIP catalogue record for this book is available from the British Library.

Typeset by Onyx Publishing of Notebook Group Limited.

This book is dedicated to my family, as well as all the women in leadership, business owners, and leaders out there who are currently struggling with finding their purpose in life.

PRAISE FOR CANDACE MAE AND
HEAVEN WITHIN

Powerfully poignant and deeply intimate, *Heaven Within* is an emotive and thought-provoking book that will keep your attention page after page. Candace Mae shares her turbulent life story that will inspire you to live your best life.

Heaven Within is a comprehensive guide that seeks to equip leaders in the workplace to live out their life's calling with resilience empowered by the Holy Spirit. This book promises a transformation in your business, mindset, and relationship with Christ. It will teach you how to purge negative thoughts and emotions and to replace them with truth based on biblical principles. This book is for anyone who finds themselves stuck in life and wants to break free to new life.

Shannon Kay McCoy, MABC, ACBC
Biblical Counseling Director, Valley Center Community Church
Author of *Help! I'm A Slave to Food*

I very much appreciate the effort and candor Candace Mae shares in this book. I believe in the speaking of LIFE to people to assist them in overcoming challenges. Candace Mae echoed Christian artist Toby Mac (Speak Life) as you spoke life to the broken hearted and loved along with providing safety is the winning recipe. Candace Mae points out that we battle not against flesh and blood (Ephesians 6:12). For Chaplains and ministers of the Gospel, you gave the remedy to assisting people in crisis *"Thankfully, Jesus modeled various approaches to helping and healing others;"* and when we take this approach with people, success is possible. This book gives a valuable look into assisting and encouraging help for those in despair.

Ben DeLeon
Rock Church Community Chaplain & Marketplace Chaplain

Candace Mae examines the powerful struggle between Good and evil, and the patterns and trends that keep us from embracing our gifts. She reveals, through her personal story, a dynamic, whole-person approach to healing, wholeness, and rising to the potential that God has created in us. You will be inspired!

Patti Cotton,
Founder, Cotton Group, Inc.

Candace Mae melds compelling personal transparency with skilled experience in working with businesses and individuals to present *Heaven Within*, propelling her readers from cultural confusion and personal weaknesses to living by vibrant, eternal truth.

She sees the workplace as a mission field and seeks to develop hope-filled disciples of Christ that have a ripple effect in influencing others. Her dependence on the person and ministry of the Holy Spirit to lead people to salvation in Christ, deliverance from bondage and fears, and sending them forth in grace is refreshing.

Dr. Rick Cross
Acorn Global Advance

Additional note from Rick:

Your book is outstanding. Thank you for your labor of love.

I was talking with a 23-year-old guy yesterday who is struggling with many of the things you describe in your book, and I was able to use your material in his life. It was a blessing to see the Lord connect the dots. God bless you!

Candace Mae's narrative is a beautiful story of God's healing and redemptive power. Through her raw and real disclosures of childhood traumas, interspersed with kingdom principles, clinical research data, and foundational guidance, she unveils the pathway that led to her being healed, becoming whole, and sustaining a fruitful life. It's a must read for any wounded heart seeking recovery.

Carol J. Clayton, Director
RSL Builders Affordable Housing, Street Ministry,
Life Transition Centers

Heaven Within is extremely informative and transformational. The lessons and stories touched me deeply and equipped me with the resources to better understand my client's needs. This book has provided me with tools to aid me in how best to speak life into my clients and point them to hope in God. I highly recommend this book to others.

Maria Salas
Cosmetologist, Valley Cuts Salon

Candace Mae's passion to help others experience wholeness and God's purpose for their lives is obvious in every page of this book. Her chapters are filled with thought-provoking nuggets that make you stop and really examine the actions of your life in a different light.

Gary Khan
Pastor and Author

The past few days I've been reading *Heaven Within Restoring Wholeness for Better Leadership*. It just changed me inside. It really made me look within. Without a doubt, the book is life-changing.

Being raised by a father who was a member of the Klu Klux Klan, in contrast to a mother who chose a life of diversity and inclusion, Candace Mae writes about being torn between a life of bigotry and a life of hope in her new book *Heaven Within*. This book will inspire you to always lean towards hope.

Pamela Mabry
Founder of Luke 4:18 Ministries
Host of Break Free Podcast

This is a fascinating story of hope and love. Not only will *Heaven Within* help you to become an outstanding leader, but also an exceptionally compassionate person.

Rachael Jayne Groover
Founder of The Awakened School

Candace Mae's deep faith shines forth upon her face, throughout her whole persona and from the pages of *Heaven Within: Restoring Wholeness for Better Leadership*. In this book, she shares the many lessons she has learned from her own journey and the challenges of her life, in order to inspire, equip and encourage her readers.

Bobbie Ann Cole
Christian writer, speaker and writing teacher

Candace Mae is incredibly unique in her ability to blend faith, science, and consciousness and advocate for humanities wellbeing. One of the wonderful things is she gives such amazing resources and gifts that help you reflect on the lessons in the book. If you are looking for a way to ignite your spirit and find heaven within, read this book!

Cory Sanchez
Founder, Mojo Global Marketing

I had the opportunity to meet with Candace Mae on a business project, and I was immediately struck by Candace Mae's compassion, love for the Lord and the excitement she has about sharing her faith. When

Candace Mae offered me to read her new book, *Heaven Within: Restoring Wholeness for Better Leadership*, I eagerly said yes. As a former Associate Pastor of the Vineyard Church Phoenix and as Founder of New Destiny Marketing, LLC I am always looking for help aligning my Christian faith to that of being an entrepreneur. Candace Mae's book is an excellent resource as she speaks about love and authenticity. I am proud to endorse both Candace Mae and her book that is helping me to be a much more effective Christian leader and the truth we should all follow, showing love in every situation.

Karen Roane
Owner, New Destiny Marketing, LLC

Candace Mae, you put a lot of effort and extra care with a lot of attention to detail into your work and it's obvious that's what you do is very important. You give 120% to your work ethic. And I admire that, and that you like to help others, and you care about them, and you take the time to be there for them.

Julia Wilcox
Logistics and Transportation Manager, Freight Connections

Candace Mae, I am very encouraged by your continuous desire to work and to improve who you are, and how you can help others and your tenacity to keep going on the fight to which God has called you.

Debra Van Essen
VE Financial

Candace Mae you are amazing. After suffering a major stroke on December 9, 2020, you have come back with energy and a drive that are just astounding. I get tired just watching. You are an author. You are in the midst of a huge marketing campaign. You have multiple podcast interviews. You're a Marketplace Chaplain, and a prayer warrior. And all the while you're building your own business, then taking care of your family. My friend, job well done.

Carol Clayton
Director, RSL Builders Affordable Housing

Candace Mae, I love how you use your intelligence, your energy, your education, your love for people, your drive your desires, everything, and allow God to use that to do the things that you're doing with your books and the coaching and training, and all of these. What you're doing is hard. You're a true entrepreneur, and a lot of people need an agency. I'm speaking on the fact that I use an agency to do what you're doing - but you're doing it on the power of God. And you are a very successful person with more fruits on their way to you. You have such a delightful personality. It's just so awesome to see God in you - that you're allowing God to bring all this out through you, and that you're allowing God to fulfill His plan for you. It's obvious that you know he's got a plan for you, and you're right there walking in step with His plan. I'm just so encouraged by you.

Sheryl Lewis
Vice President Sales and Consulting at HUB International of California Insurance Services, Inc.

Deborah and I use the same words. This is the powerful word, tenacity. That was the word that came to mind: tenacity. Your willingness to learn a skill that takes a lot, and to overcome where you come from. You are an overcomer - you ARE an overcomer. you haven't *been* an overcomer - you ARE an overcomer! That is a huge thing. I see you have great perseverance. I see your faith growing on a regular basis. Faith doesn't grow in the easy times. It grows in the hard times. I've seen your faith growing immensely. I offer you this verse; this verse came to mind when thinking of you: *"David encouraged and strengthened himself in the Lord."* And that's who I see you to be. So, that is the verse that I see as your life government.

Cindy Marks
Trustee, Modesto City Schools Board of Education

CONTENTS

PROLOGUE

We all have a story. Have you taken time to reflect on yours; on where you've been and where you're headed? We each enter this world naked, with just our souls, and we leave this world the same. What happens during our journey here is depicted on our tombstones by a mere dash. What will your dash represent?

As a parent, we not only think about our own dash (life), but the dashes of all the lives we've brought into this world—yet we cannot control those dashes (the life experiences and stories that fill the lives of our loved ones). Rather, each of us is solely responsible for our own choices, and it can be challenging to distinguish where our responsibility begins and ends.

So, how do we let go and allow our grown children to live their lives, and yet still be responsible for supporting and loving them? Simply, we must speak life and hope into them while realizing and accepting that the ultimate choice of how they choose to live is theirs.

We provide guidance while they are young and we always love them, and yet we don't indulge them and give too much comfort when they choose unhealthy lifestyles, especially those involving drugs or violence.

Suppose your grown children, as adults, refuse to embrace the help available to them: in this scenario, we must let them fully experience the consequences of their choices while still loving them. We are each responsible for our own decisions and our own lives. Like with a drowning victim, we must first stabilize ourselves, wait for the individual to reach exhaustion, and then grab and pull them to safety when they need us most, unable to fight and pull us down with them. This is similar to adults with an addiction (and sometimes those with mental health challenges) who refuse to get the support they need: an intervention may be staged, but it's usually only effective once the person realizes and accepts that they need help.

Some parents find it bittersweet to watch their children grow into adults: witnessing them struggling to find themselves and get established financially or dealing with a health challenge is a bitter experience, while watching them grow into that career that provides a strong foundation for themselves and their family is a sweet one. After having multiple children myself, I, too, am in the process of watching several different scenarios play out.

How do you feel when you see your grown children flounder? You may have had the financial ability to pay for your child's education and may have even influenced their career by providing key connections for that ideal career position, and in that case, you may tend to take full credit for your grown child's financial stability and success. Are you that parent who boasts, *My children are doing so well; I must have done something right?*

When your children struggle and everything is uphill, you may feel as I did on occasion: like others judge you as a bad person or incompetent parent based on the evidence of your grown child's struggle. But that's not necessarily true! Do not accept those labels: we are made in the image of God; we have intrinsic value. Grasp hold of how God sees you and hold onto God's Truth. As a woman of faith, I know that I am the daughter of the King of Kings. God lives in me: His seed is in me, and I was made in His image. I am of mighty worth, and so are my children and grandchildren—and so are you! Acknowledging the truth of who we are when we have a relationship with Jesus Christ as our Lord and Savior solidifies the fact that our behaviors do not define us, nor do they determine our worth as humans. We must realize that our behavior is not who we are: we— each of us and our children—are all far more than our behavior, and accordingly, we must learn to separate the person from the behavior. Behavior is a result of beliefs—oftentimes beliefs that are subconscious, of which we are not yet aware.

Later, we'll be diving deeper into these topics and will explore the Truth: that we all have choices. Though our options are vast, we may feel that there are very few options to choose from; our subconscious beliefs restrict what choices we see as being before us. Hence, I believe our work in this life is to uncover the lies in our subconscious beliefs that we hold onto and replace them with the Truth of our Creator. Only then will we see the abundant range of choices available to us.

There is power in our beliefs, so choose wisely: we can choose to ask God, our Master Designer, to guide all areas of our path, including those of our family and business. He will straighten your path when you practice His Presence in your daily life.

I make the daily decision to ask God to help me to awaken the hidden beliefs in my subconscious. Even as I wrote this book, I developed a broader and deeper perspective, gaining an even more vital awareness of my ability to choose. In fact, I wrote the initial manuscript for this book in May 2020, during the COVID-19 pandemic, and six months into reviewing the manuscript, I experienced a twelve-week series of significant, deep breakthroughs in my unconscious beliefs. These breakthroughs brought profound insight into the truths and deeper understandings that I had already begun writing about in these pages.

In this book, I would like to be a bridge for you to Christ—or, should you already have a close relationship with Christ, to help you to further your authentic discipleship with Christ in and through your business. I'd like to help you to discover how to engage the Holy Spirit in your business and integrate it into your team and processes so you can keep your ultimate focus on the presence of Jesus Christ in all things—even our businesses. The workplace is the largest mission field, and as authentic disciples of Jesus Christ empowered by the Holy Spirit, we can be the vessels to touch the lives of others with the love of Christ, thereby changing the world with ripple effects. God wants our businesses to thrive; God wants us to put Him first; God wants to change lives through His love. Hence, we must learn to lead with love!

Having had such deep breakthroughs in my beliefs, I was able to revisit these pages and seep in even more wisdom—so join me on the journey of my soul's reflection as I share the lessons I have learned about how God majestically and holistically designed us as spiritual and emotional beings gifted with a physical body, and what we need to be aware of to have breakthroughs. We will cover systemic family issues that have been passed down through generations and carry over into business and society at large, personal growth lessons (a prerequisite to authentic and compassionate leadership development, since leadership growth begins with personal growth and inner victories), and breaking the stigma behind mental and emotional health. (Our complete health requires a holistic approach to physical, mental, emotional, and spiritual health; we're spiritual beings having a physical experience, at the end of the day, and so our energetic and emotional state directly impacts our physical health and should not be shamed, suppressed, or denied.)

Join me as I share my story and the lessons learned along the way. May they help you to reflect on your life, remind you that you're not alone, and shed some wisdom on how to have your own breakthroughs so you can move forward in life and leadership.

Notably, should you be fully committed to this journey of internal transformation (which I hope you are!), please take this moment to go download this book's companion guide, which you can find at https://workbook-hw.candacemae.com/. This has an exercise for you to complete at the end of every chapter so you can fully absorb and begin to apply the content of each chapter. Then, once you do this, proceed to the next chapter and repeat!

Now, let's get started.

CHAPTER 1:
DISCOVER TRUTH

P EOPLE NEED TO KNOW THAT they are heard before they can hear others. After all, don't you feel that way? If you're upset, don't you need to feel heard before you can absorb what others are saying to you? People need to know they are valued; that they matter. I need to feel valued, and so do you.

People also need to know that they are safe before they can grow: no one who is in great pain can grow into something better until they are first loved just as they are, without needing to be better. If you trace the growth of a successful thought leader who came from a background of pain, you'll find that at some point during their journey, they were loved by someone who believed in them; they found a mentor (even if it was an author or podcast or another source) who encouraged their soul and breathed life and hope into them.

You matter. *People* matter. *All* people matter: every race; every color.

You are also not your behavior; rather, your behavior is a reaction to the pain you are in. Further, your thoughts are not you; you are more than your thoughts. Instead, you are God's essence. You are enough just as you are: God created you; God conceived you. You are beautiful and embody great energy. You are immensely powerful and were created with the essence of love. (Notably, "essence" is defined as the core nature or most important qualities of a person or thing; the permanent, as contrasted with the accidental, element of being.)

You and I have been deceived about our identity. A great lie has been veiled over the world. This world is full of pain, on every continent and in every country, city, town, neighborhood, and home. You and I (along with all of mankind) have been deceived about our identities and the essence of who we are, and those lies have been passed down generationally ever since the great fall. The past cannot be changed. You *can*, however, be awakened to the Truth. You can choose to know the Truth and to live another way. And that is exactly what this book is here to awaken you to.

Life may be hard at times, but God is here with you, waiting for you to accept Him into your life. You were created to live in this world with power and dominion over all things. The earth was designed to be your comfort: sun, wind, and rain, with stars to entertain and guide you, water to drink, and oceans for food and resources. The natural earth was created with everything in abundance so you would have no worries. God has already fulfilled your physical, earthly needs via your environment—and He is now waiting with open arms for you to allow Him to fulfill your spiritual needs.

Finding your way back to God is the key to peace and Truth, and God has placed a seed in your heart to seek the Truth.

This book was written for each of you; for the masses; for all people. It was written for my family and loved ones to help them to awaken to the Truth.

And this book was written to give you hope; for you to realize that you are not alone. I hope that you will be able to relate to my God-inspired stories, and as I share my stories, I pray you will tear away the veil that is covering your eyes and preventing you from seeing the Truth, leaving you able to see your self, situation, and family clearly.

It is possible to break free from the systemic biases and problems of this world; I have grown and broken free, for the most part! There is, however, constant growth and more awareness to achieve; I will continue to grow until I die. In mind of this, I want to show you how I healed and encourage you to embrace healing and continual growth.

My goal is to teach others how to find their own voice and path out of bondage; to help people to move from the pain of feeling broken, damaged, ugly, and shameful and come to know that *there is more*; that there is great love inside themselves. There is great Knowing inside each of us, and the essence of your soul is Great Love. You are a powerful, energetic being, as you were designed and created in God's image. God is the Alpha and Omega; the Beginning and the End.

> *Behold, I am coming soon, and My reward is with Me, to give to each one according to what he has done. I am the Alpha and the Omega, the First and the Last, the Beginning and the End. Blessed are those who wash their robes, so that they may have the right to the tree of life and may enter the city by its gates.*
> —Revelations 22:13

We were created to see the beauty in nature; in plants; in flowers; in animals; to know that God made each of us even more beautiful and more powerful than the animals and nature. We were created to have power and dominion over this world.

However, we have been deceived and not taught the Truth about who we really are: our ancestors were lied to by Satan, which ultimately destroyed our innocence and awareness of the Truth of our identity—and when our ancestors listened to the lies of Satan and disobeyed God's command, we lost our awareness of God's Truth as the default setting of our mind, instead taking on Satan's Innate Nature (sin). This limited our awareness of our power and tricked us into believing we were independent of God.

We became like a mighty elephant who was chained at birth to a stake which he couldn't break free from: as the elephant grows, his strength grows, too, ultimately leaving him able to easily break that chain that has constrained him since birth—and yet because the elephant was taught from a young age that he had no choice and was destined to live chained, he doesn't even try to break free. The grown elephant has been raised to believe he has no choice—that the chain cannot be broken—and so he doesn't try to push the boundaries. If the grown elephant knew the potential of his power, however, he would easily break free from the chain that constricts him.

It's time to awaken to the Truth; to remove the veil from your eyes that has been hiding it. It's time to awaken to your potential and to break free; to become conscious of the power inside of you; to become awakened to who God created you to be!

I imagine that as God contemplated the creation of man, He asked Himself, "What if they could choose? Would they choose me, or would they choose to be independent? Would they choose to be their own god?" God allowed our ancestors to experience innocence and purity in His presence, and He also planted a seed within man's soul that would allow him the ability to find God if his awareness of Him was lost. We are created in God's image *with the ability to choose.*

This was a great approach: according to Genesis 2:15-18, the first man was created and brought into the world and granted daily time with God so he could intimately know God. Then, God introduced the man to his ability to choose by instructing him to eat anything from the beautiful garden in which he lived, except the tree that grants the Knowledge of Good and Evil. As long as man chose to obey God's instruction, he would continue to experience pure joy, love, and companionship directly with God daily; but if he decided to eat the fruit from the forbidden tree, he would lose his innocence, direct connection, and awareness of God. The Bible describes the loss of connection to God as death.

Hence, when man chose to do something different from what God instructed, essentially disobeying God's guidance, that man and all his ancestors were blinded to God and His ways. Man's own ego took over by default, and we began to be led by our five physical senses, which are tied to this earth, while man's spiritual senses became limited. Life became a long journey—difficult at best—because man's ego (i.e., his self-esteem or self-importance) had become self-focused. (According to psychoanalysis, the ego is the part of the mind that mediates between the conscious and the unconscious and is responsible for reality testing and a sense of personal identity; meanwhile, philosophy—more specifically, metaphysics—views the ego as a conscious, thinking object.)

This world under the reign of man's ego experiences extreme pain and hurt. Man has become self-focused and absorbed in pain, the physical senses now ruling the human experience. It is difficult for the majority of people to grasp spiritual truths; that is, the things we cannot see, smell, taste, touch, or hear. However, God anticipated this loss of connection and made a way for us to return to His companionship. God clearly states in Deuteronomy 4:29, Proverbs 8:17, Jeremiah 29:13, Matthew 7:7, Luke 11:9, and Acts 17:24-28, "When they seek me with their whole heart, they will find Me." Here,

God is patient and clearly states that He will wait for people to seek Him.

Do you recall who Satan is? Satan was the most beautiful angel God created, in charge of all music and worship—until he decided he wanted to be worshipped and so defied God. Satan led a group of fallen angels to follow him and came to this realm (Earth) to deceive man so that man would worship Satan. It was Satan who tricked Eve into eating the fruit from the Tree of the Knowledge of Good and Evil, who then persuaded Adam to do the same. This was in defiance of God's command not to eat the fruit of that tree.

Satan tricked Eve by telling her if she ate the fruit of the Tree of the Knowledge of Good and Evil (which God forbid), she wouldn't die (as God told Adam he would), but instead would become wiser, like God, essentially becoming a god. Eve ate the fruit and then convinced Adam to do the same.

It is because our ancestors decided to eat that fruit that our world entered the fallen state it is in, with our awareness focused on physical, egocentric matter. Our relationship and connection to God have both been broken, all because of a lie. By listening to the lies of Satan, Adam gave his God-given power and dominion in this world to Satan.

Satan became the prince of this realm and man's conscious awareness of God was broken. It is a sad tragedy, but the Truth: we are born into this fallen world and are handed down these lies through generations—the lie that God is a myth; that Satan is a myth; that man can do all things independently; that it's mind over matter. We curse God's name, but not Satan's.

Satan takes what God made as good and twists it for evil, and so Christians must embrace the Truth, power, and birthright in Christ. Stop believing the lies of Satan, take complete ownership of the gifts

God has given us, and use them to give God glory and reveal His Truth.

I tell you the truth, anyone who has faith in me will do what I have been doing. He will do even greater things than these, because I am going to the Father.
—John 14:12

God designed man to live on a spiritual plane as His companion, yet when man chose to eat from the Tree of Knowledge of Good and Evil, our spiritual Knowing was hidden (veiled) from us. Man wanted to be all-knowing—to be like God—and for that choice, we would have to start our evolution at the physical level. We chose to be our own god, so God granted us that scenario—yet he was kind enough to hide the Tree of Eternal Life, for God knew our ego's nature was self-centered and we would hurt others to preserve ourselves. It was because of this that God said that we must learn to live in the physical realm so we could understand our limits, remaining focused on our five senses (relative to the physical world). We would have to farm the land to eat, and eventually, we would learn humility: that we did not know all there was; that we were not God. When we become tired of forcing survival in the physical world, we start to seek something more.

God placed that yearning and hunger within us, calling us to find Him. This is like a game of hide-and-seek: while you are hiding, you know someone is looking for you. However, sometimes, you hide and wonder if they have given up seeking. In the same way, it is not a fun exercise for God to wait for you to find Him, though it is required. When you ate from the Tree of Knowledge of Good and Evil, your ego was created. Your ego believes you are all you need; that you are the center of your world. Your ego is what drives the pain, selfishness, and narcissistic behavior you exhibit. You, therefore, must first come to terms (through humility) with the fact that you do not have all the answers; that *no* man has all the answers. Only when you have exhausted your own resources will you seek God.

CHAPTER 2:
WHAT MATTERS: HEAVEN WITHIN

LIFE HAS SO MUCH MORE to offer when we have a relationship with God. God is relentlessly making opportunities for you and me to see Him; to ask Him to be known to us; and when we seek a relationship with God and acknowledge Him as our Divine Creator, God begins transforming our awareness in such a way where we can suddenly see the ego's lies that kept God hidden from our grasp. However, to receive the total abundance God provides, man must first choose to submit his ego and embrace God as his Creator.

People are constantly drowning in confusion, hate, anger, miscommunication, shame, guilt, and unworthiness; people are malicious because they are blind and don't know what to do. Many people feel unlovable, our society having thwarted and perverted the meaning of love when our very spiritual essence is love.

Love is a quality, characteristic, and verb; love is active and caring; love embraces our entire being, using all of our senses (both the physical and spiritual). Our five physical senses allow us to engage and enjoy our physical realm on Earth, although we were also created with other substances that our society hasn't yet fully embraced. God designed and gifted us with faculties that enhance our ability to express our essence of love, and through our physical senses, love can be expressed in the physical realm by way of pleasure. *True* love, however, does not reside in the physical senses: love is of the spiritual realm, and so love is elusive to most people, since they are living solely in the physical realm. God created us to live in more than one realm at a time: He gifted us with several faculties that most people know little about how to use.

Our six faculties include memory, reason, perception, imagination, intuition, and will—and when people discover how to use these faculties, they will find God more easily. God is the essence of True Love and includes the qualities of all these six faculties, which all come from our divine energy source. This is where our power lies. You must seek God with your whole heart, and then you will find Him; you must discover and learn how to control these faculties.

There were also false prophets among the people, just as there will be false teachers among you.
—Peter 2:1

Be careful, my friend, for mighty things can be done simply by understanding God's design of man and this world. God created laws to keep the world functioning.

Our default mode is ego-driven: the ego is self-centered, and so when we stay in the ego-driven mode, we use base behaviors that are self-centered and self-focused for self-gain and typically center around our five senses rather than on a spiritual focus. Here, we inadvertently serve ourselves at the cost of others—even those who we say we love.

To stop exhibiting base behaviors and instead start exhibiting those with higher frequencies, we must awaken our six faculties. Here, we must self-care—and when I say self-care, I don't mean the physical pleasure of getting a massage or your nails and hair done (though that is enjoyable and self-care for the physical body), but self-care at a deeper, more emotional and spiritual level, such as practicing coping skills like meditation (remember to download this book's companion guide!), focusing on all things good and praiseworthy, and observing our thoughts. Self-care involves capturing our thoughts, expelling their negative beliefs, and realigning them with Truth. Self-care involves recognizing the fact that we are not our past, nor are we limited by our current circumstances, as well as the fact that we can use our six faculties to imagine, design, and create a better life. We are spiritual beings having an energetic experience in our physical bodies with the ability to create or co-create with God.

There is much power in our faculties. They stand alone, and when we understand our God-created faculties and His universal laws, there is power. Be careful not to misuse the power of these God-designed gifts, however.

Having a relationship with Christ is essential for the proper alignment of these gifts: through the guidance of Christ's Holy Spirit dwelling within us, we are granted advice on how to use these gifts. Without the direction of Christ's Spirit, these gifts alone can easily lead people down the wrong path—a path where the ego rules and power is misused. Like all things designed for good, they can be used for evil in the hands of the wrong person. That is Satan's consistent process: to get you to deny God and believe you can do all things without Him.

Satan has come to steal and lie.

When we become aware that we are spiritual beings having a physical human experience, we will be able to tap into our spiritual senses—and much like the physical senses, God created us with spiritual insights that are best guided and used when connected to God and His Spirit.

These spiritual (energetic) senses fall under the faculty of intuition, and include having a:

1. Clear (spiritual) knowing.
2. Clear (spiritual) vision.
3. Clear (spiritual) hearing.
4. Clear (spiritual) smell.
5. Clear (spiritual) taste.
6. Clear emotional feelings, from others and our surroundings.
7. Clear physical feelings that we take on from others.
8. Clear touch (whereby we detect facts about the things we touch).
9. Clear intellect (whereby we suddenly know facts about others or things without knowing how we know it).

Many churches and Christians are afraid to acknowledge these spiritual gifts because man has discovered these and labeled them as "psychic" or "new-age phenomena"—but the truth is that Satan is a deceiver—a counterfeit—and has taken God's design and twisted it, removing the Truth. I believe our ego is what drives sin (simply a term to define our defiance toward God and Satan's Innate Nature).

It is time for Christians to fully embrace their divine power through Christ's Holy Spirit. We are charged with the mission to awaken others to the Truth.

But what do I mean by this? Let's take a moment to answer these questions by revisiting Christianity's origins, rather than making the assumption that we all already possess the same level of understanding. Understanding these fundamentals is essential to having a relationship with Jesus Christ and becoming awakened to the foundational truth of the God of the Universe; the God above all gods; our Creator.

First, notice I said, "God above all gods." Perhaps you believe that God is God, regardless of who we each understand Him to be. Some believe that all paths lead to one God. However, this is not true; all paths do *not* lead to the one true God.

Furthermore, it is notable that our Creator is often referred to as the "Unknown God"—and, accordingly, many religions use objects to pray or make sacrifices to, while others regard the figurehead or founder of their religion to be a great saint; indeed, many think Jesus Christ is just a good man or a saint, as is common in many other religions. Alternatively, many don't believe the Bible to be God's Word and an instruction manual for us, even though scientists today are continually discovering historical facts and scientific evidence that proves the stories in the Bible to be wholly accurate. To go back to our initial point, while in the Christian faith Jesus Christ is somewhat of a figurehead, He never took credit for establishing a religion; rather, He pointed to God as the Creator of the Universe and the Creator of Man, simply stating that He (Jesus) had come to restore man in his relationship with God. So, unlike the figureheads of other religions, Jesus Christ never focuses on himself; rather, he clearly states that He was brought into this world through a virgin birth conceived by God so that He would not be under the "fallen state" of the world. Instead, He came into this world fully connected to God, with the purpose to be with and connect with man; to live the human experience, take upon himself the sins of man, and show man how to restore his relationship to God.

To review the story many may be familiar with: God is a righteous God, so for justice to be served, Jesus Christ came to be the scapegoat. Hence, He suffered separation from God during his time on the cross and during the three days His body was dead. Then, He rose from the dead, overcoming the sinful state so that those who believe in Jesus Christ as the son of God would come to know God in a true relationship again, as originally designed before the Great Fall. After rising from death, Christ left this earthly realm and returned to the heavenly realm to be with Father—and in doing so, Jesus Christ was able to send His Holy Spirit to dwell in those who believe in Him.

> *For God so loved the world that he gave his one and only Son, that whoever believes in him shall not perish but have eternal life.*
> —John 3:16

Indeed, the Spirit, when it dwells inside man, begins its good work within man: it gives us a direct connection with God so we can have clear Knowing from God. The Spirit transforms Satan's Innate Nature (sin) in us and replaces it with Christ's Nature—and as we become conscious to the Holy Spirit within us, we are transformed through the Spirit's power, God's innate essence of love beginning to root deep inside us so that our outward actions begin to reflect this inner state of love.

> *And I pray that you, being rooted and established in love,[18] may have power, together with all the Lord's holy people, to grasp how wide and long and high and deep is the love of Christ,[19] and to know this love that surpasses knowledge—that you may be filled to the measure of all the fullness of God.*
> —Ephesians 3:16-21

When Jesus rose from death, he said he was leaving this earthly realm to be with the Father so that His Spirit could come to dwell within those who believe in Him, in turn receiving spiritual power and comfort that they would not otherwise have had access to.

Many people, however, have begun to seek spiritual ways without acknowledging our Creator and the sacrifice of Jesus Christ to restore our relationship with Him. Many people have begun to agree that we are spiritual beings and they seek to find spiritual power, and yet they do it without acknowledging our Creator. Be careful with this!

Beloved, do not believe every spirit, but test the spirits to see whether they are from God, for many false prophets have gone out into the world.
—John 4:1

God's principles and universal laws are true, and to add to this, God clearly tells us in His Word that we must accept a relationship with His son Jesus Christ and acknowledge our belief in His son to the world—which we initially do through water baptism. Notably, the baptism of the Holy Spirit is the process by which the Holy Spirit comes to dwell within us, in turn granting us the power to live spiritually and to hear from God, rather than being driven by our physical nature. It is through the Holy Spirit dwelling in us that we receive His gifts and our lives begin to manifest the fruits of the Holy Spirit (love, joy, peace, patience, gentleness, goodness, faith, meekness, and self-control).

You did not choose me, but I chose you and appointed you so that you might go and bear fruit—fruit that will last—and so that whatever you ask in My name the Father will give you.[17]
This is my command: Love each other.
—John 15:16-17

Our key lesson (and first instruction) out of all of this? The essence of God and His Holy Spirit is love: when the Holy Spirit comes to dwell within us as believers in Jesus Christ, we begin to be transformed from the inside out so that love is manifested in our words and actions. This is a transformational growth process that an authentic disciple of Jesus Christ undergoes.

Hence, when we take on all that the Bible tells us as Truth and initiate a baptism of the Holy Spirit, we begin to receive a new understanding of love. This starts with the inner state of our mind.

Please take a moment to review the chart below and to compare the attributes of the Spirit (the essence of love) against the sinful nature that is derived from the fallen state of man, whereby we focus on the flesh and our physical nature by default.

Area of Behavior	The Spirit Produces love... (Galatians 5:22-23)	The Flesh (ego) Produces sin...
Inner State of Mind	LOVE (charity; the foundation on which the others are built)	Hatred, anger, animosity, hostility, murder.
	JOY	Heaviness, sorrow, misery, depression.
	PEACE	Strife, contention, restlessness, anxiety.
Attitude Towards Others	LONGSUFFERING (patience)	Impatience, fretfulness, hastiness.
	GENTLENESS (kindness/benignity)	Pushiness, harshness, quarrelsomeness.
	GOODNESS (mildness)	Wickedness, jealousy, sorcery, immorality.
Demonstrate Trust in the Lord	FAITH	Doubt, mistrust, unbelief, apprehension.
	MEEKNESS (modesty)	Pride, selfish ambition, intolerance.
	SELF-CONTROL (contingency, chastity)	Addictions, angry outbursts, unrestraint.

While man was created in God's image and each man has God's seed within him, it isn't until we accept Jesus Christ as our Savior and we receive the baptism of the Holy Spirit that we receive adequate spiritual power to live by faith. It is through the power of the Holy Spirit that we can live our life through spiritual awareness and make choices founded in love, rather than the default behavior of the flesh shown in the table above. The Spirit does the work within us to transform us into the essence of love; it's not something we can do and sustain on our own.

Notice in the chart above that love includes our inner state of mind, attitude towards others, and demonstration of our trust in the Lord: by default (from the fallen state of the world), we tend to respond with the fleshly responses written in the third column. I am certain you can relate to each of those responses. It is difficult to respond with love as our *first* response—*unless* the Spirit empowers us.

Hence, I encourage you to accept Christ as your Savior and to establish a personal relationship with Christ's Holy Spirit. You will never be alone in this troubled world if you do so, as you will have Christ's Spirit dwelling within you, constantly guiding you. It is in light of all of the above that this book endeavors to help you to become an authentic disciple of Jesus Christ, discover love, joy, and peace beyond understanding, restore your relationship with God, and understand and embrace your purpose in life. Realize that life is difficult for all of us, and while a relationship with Christ will not take away its difficulties, it will give us a spiritual companion that dwells with us, giving us the power to embrace and overcome this world and the challenges we face within it. As we face life's struggles, God's Spirit will use those circumstances to bring about good in our lives.

> *The thief comes only to steal and kill and destroy; I have come so that they may have life, and may have it abundantly.*
> —John 10:10

Think about this: each person who has an influential role in the narrative concerning integrity has endured a path of hardship and struggle. You may not realize it as you see them now in their glory, but it is true: everyone has their own story of trial, error, and overcoming.

It was when they learned humility (i.e., that they needed others) that they were able to get farther.

Everyone has their own story. We do not realize this, though; our ego is so self-centered that we do not think that anyone else understands us: we cater to our own needs at the expense of those around us in accordance with our natural fallen state. Only those who have been awakened to some degree can lead and teach others about the two conditions of life: first, we have the original design of abundance and co-creators with God, living in innocence and love; and second, after the choice to be our own god was made came the ego: self-centered with a scarcity mindset, whereby loneliness and pain are the default state for each of us.

People are hurting. The human ego, when focused only on the senses, is base, vulgar, selfish, and abusive: fathers fail to provide for their children and their wives; mothers strive to support their offspring but grow weary, angry, and depressed, sometimes beginning to abuse others out of self-preservation. You were not designed or meant to be alone in this world, however: God made us for His companionship; God decided we needed another made in our own image to connect with in this world on the physical plane. You were designed to create. You want more because God *made* you want more: to experience love; laughter; a life full of expression. Yet without God and the peace God brings, you are afraid; scared. You seek out companionship with other humans, but they are cruel, self-centered, and use you to profit themselves. Therefore, in Matthew 18:19-20, God tells those who have found Him to only partner and marry with another who has found Him. Why? Because when you both know and seek God, there is greater power between you.

Again, truly, I tell you that if two of you on earth agree about anything they ask for, it will be done for them by my Father in heaven. For where two or

three gathers in my name, there am I with them.
—Matthew 18:19-20

God's Spirit, once awakened in us, changes our desires and our values, and when you partner with someone who does not know God, they are controlled by the ego and are constrained to the ways of the flesh.

The acts of the flesh are obvious: sexual immorality, impurity and debauchery; idolatry and witchcraft; hatred, discord, jealousy, fits of rage, selfish ambition, dissensions, factions and envy; drunkenness, orgies, and the like. I warn you, as I did before, that those who live like this will not inherit the kingdom of God.
—Galatians 5:19-21

God asks us to be an example of His love and acceptance so they, too, can find God. Being a Spirit-filled person partnered with an ego-based person is incredibly sad, since they will not share your values, and may abuse and torment you and try to get you to turn from God and be "normal". You were not meant for this treatment, yet if you choose a path that is unequally matched spiritually, you will face consequences for your choice.

So, once you discover God's Truth with this book, begin asking God about every detail of your life. Include God in your thoughts daily. Now that you have found God, rely on God moment by moment. Talk to Him; ask Him for guidance. He will guide you. God is guiding me at this very moment. You can trust God: God is your Creator and He intimately knows you better than you know yourself. God will not fail you. Yes, it is scary for you to trust a God you cannot physically see, but He will make himself known to you. As you grow in your faith and spiritual understanding, God will be able to show you more of Him. There may be much you do not understand, and that is okay: you live in the physical world with restrictions and limitations, and a dark veil reigns on Earth, blocking God's Truth.

God is calling for His people to humble themselves; to acknowledge their sins and their ways of seeking their own ego; to confess and seek God's wisdom and guidance; to praise Him for His worthiness and provide thanksgiving for His faithfulness.

> *If my people, who are called by my name, will humble themselves and pray and seek my face and turn from their wicked ways, then I will hear from heaven, and I will forgive their sin and will heal their land.*
> —Chronicles 7:14

The power of God's presence is found in trusting Him daily, moment by moment, decision by decision. We must choose God's values and learn to live them out daily; we must understand how God designed us and what gifts and strengths God has bestowed upon us. We are each unique—similar, but unique.

Know your gift mix. There is a reason why you have the strengths and skills you do. Remember, as you work with the gifts and strengths that God gave you, God will work through you so that your work (His work) will be amplified and multiplied beyond your greatest imagination. Notably, the best way you can identify your gift mix and thus exploit your gifts to the max is by downloading my very own workbook that guides you to discovering this: *The You Factor: Your Gift Mix Workbook.* This is available for download here: https://giftmix.candacemae.com/. This workbook is packed with exercises that will help you to discover your value and guide you through questions that will help you to explore your past so you can understand your strengths. There are assessments I offer as a trainer that will shed great insight into your personality, learning style, values, motivators, and even how to understand the communication and buying styles of others so you can adjust your approach to get your ideas across—great for those of you in business!

God needs you and I to be bolder and braver. Are you willing? I am! God needs us to be vulnerable so we can share our stories of pain and challenges and how God helped us to overcome them in such a way where those stories transformed into powerful stories of God's faithfulness and power. You, like I, may have been told to never let others see your pain or they will attack—yet what God is asking of you and I requires courage. Can you be vulnerable and share how God has worked and solved miracles in your life? Will you be brave and courageous enough to share your weaknesses so that God's power can shine through?

I have God Stories—*so* many God Stories. God wants me to risk being vulnerable, and I invite you to capture and share your God Stories with the world. There are lessons in those experiences that others can learn from. Your stories, just like my stories, can (and will!) awaken others. Through hearing our stories, the masses will see the parallel troubles in their own lives and will want to experience God's transformative power; to receive and be engulfed by God's love, joy, and peace in their own lives.

If you have accepted Christ into your heart, you are now an Awakener: you are God's Light, and God's Light shines through our broken and shattered pieces. This is okay; there is no shame in being perfectly imperfect! We are more beautiful with God's Light shining and working in, with, and through us than when we are living in the darkness of the ego.

Are you willing to share your intimate stories concerning how God touches your life? I am willing. Are you willing to be vulnerable? I am. Are you willing to speak life and hope into the lives of those around you? I am willing to surrender to the Spirit of God working in, with, and through me to affect transformation in me and in the lives of those around me. This begins with you and I surrendering to the spiritual growth within us first, however.

Here are a few of my stories. These stories are shared as an example of how we are hardwired to react under fear. When fear kicks in, we cannot control how our bodies respond; it takes acute self-awareness to recognize what is happening and to overrule our systems' default reactions.

Before we proceed, however, please first refer to your companion guide (that you printed earlier) and complete the corresponding exercise as you meditate on the ideas we have already explored. Then, when you are ready, proceed to the next pages.

CHAPTER 3:
OUR BRAIN BY DESIGN

A S AN AUTHENTIC DISCIPLE OF Jesus Christ, it is important that you lead with courage, bravery, love, and forgiveness, and that you share your voice. It was my choice to be an example of someone who broke free from the lies, despite being born into an old, wicked family; an example of someone who found love in God and was able to forgive those who hurt her.

Please remember to forgive yourself and be kind to yourself. You will learn more about God's Truth and love bit by bit; layer by layer. As you experience these lessons and gain wisdom and healing, you will be tasked with the job of sharing this Truth with others. This Truth is the elixir you must bring to the rest of your family, friends, colleagues, and the world. You were born for such a time as this; a critical time of change. The world is changing; evolving. Be the Light to show the way. Be the salt that preserves and adds flavor.

We reside in a world focused on manual labor. *Do as I say. No need to educate the children; they are workers.* Workers for what? *To tend the land; to feed us.* But what then? *A cycle of working the land, growing crops, and hunting for food.* This was the experience of my father, a child of the south born in 1923. His father—my grandfather—was born in 1870. My father was the youngest of fourteen (originally fifteen, but one passed away within three days of their birth). A third-grade education was all he was allowed, and his siblings and parents forced him, like the other children, to stay home and farm the land. Third grade is for those who are only eight years of age, around when the conscious begins to develop. If you stop a person's growth before their conscious develops, you control the beliefs and behavior of that person. This saddens me deeply, and as a result of this injustice, I saw firsthand how bigotry and hate were passed down from generation to generation. Someone *must* awaken such people; otherwise, they will remain ignorant of the truth. How will they know otherwise?

I sought God out during each difficult phase of life, and in doing so, God was able to mold me; to grow and stretch me out of my comfort zone. I sought God while I was in pain, asking for His guidance; for the next best step. At times, I insisted on having my way. I begged God. However, God's way is always the best way, and so we must stop choosing good and wait for God's best! I know it is scary to surrender your choice, but once you build your trust in God, know that God has your back and manifests in the form of pure joy and serenity. You and I are human, perfectly imperfect, and so you and I need God—and God is here for all of us.

The brain is a beautiful design and is insanely powerful. We have defenses that automatically engage to protect us. The amygdala (a filter or gatekeeper for the reptilian brain) is one of those beautiful designs: God designed it to quickly kick in with a fight-or-flight reflex to preserve us from danger. The amygdala is recognized as a component of the limbic system and plays important roles in arousal, autonomic responses, fear, emotional responses, hormonal secretions (e.g., adrenaline, epinephrine, and norepinephrine), and memory. It is best known, however, for its role in the processing of fear. If we have ongoing or repeated threats in life, our brains become hypersensitive to cues that remind us of those traumatic experiences. We can then have intense emotional reactions to cues, and our reptilian brain will activate our flight, fight, freeze, or fawn survival responses.

Take some time to pause and observe the sensations in your body: what do you notice as you scan from your head down to your toes? Do you have tension-filled tight spots in your shoulders, as if the weight of the world is on them? Do you have numbing in your fingers or toes? Cramping in your calves? Sharp pain in your lower back? Remember, we were designed with three central points in our brain: the reptilian mind (with a fight-or-flight auto-response), which engages with our first interactions with our world and registers if we are safe or not; the limbic system, which controls our emotions and memories; and the frontal cortex, which is where our logical functioning occurs.

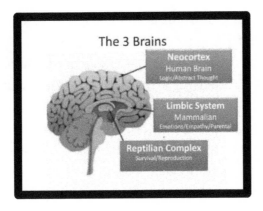

(Image printed with permission from http://soulguru.com/triune-brain)

We have a built-in thirty-second response time from the moment of stimuli to our reaction. While thirty seconds may not sound like a lot of time, it's long enough for us to intelligently respond—and when we develop self-awareness, we have the ability to become aware of those thirty seconds between stimulus/stimuli and response and to choose how we *want* to respond—at least to some degree.

Still not convinced of the power of thought, manifestation, and the fight-or-flight response? The other day, my twenty-three-year-old daughter and I took a nature walk through a wooded area behind our home when suddenly, there was a skunk in the path, and it was *not* scurrying away. We kept walking in the direction of the skunk when I suddenly became afraid that the skunk was going to jump on me or spray me. I totally froze: I literally couldn't move. I screamed and stood there. Rachel laughed a knowing laugh and pushed me to get me moving. The skunk finally did move, and we kept walking. What stood out to me was the strength of the reaction that overtook my body.

The freaky part? Rachel had told me before we headed out on our walk that the night before, she had been walking the trail at dusk alone when some black animal came out of the woods and started following her. It scared her, and she turned around and started jumping up and down, shouting for it to go away and not follow her. She spent hours on Google trying to figure out what the animal was. So, naturally, while on our walk, I was thinking about that little black creature when the skunk appeared on our pathway.

Two things are interesting about this story: first, I had been thinking about a creature coming onto my path when one appeared; and second, this distinctly demonstrates the power of the reptilian brain: I was frozen with panic, unable to move.

Now, hopefully you are coming to a great realization concerning the magnitude of the power and design of the body. While understanding the principles of how our brains work is incredible, having the experiences right there and then is what is truly amazing. I'd been studying the brain, how we create new beliefs, and what holds us back for years—and now here was an event that brought home everything I was studying!

While our reactive response is a gift and strength for our survival, let's be reminded that any strength taken too far becomes a weakness and no longer serves us well. We cannot live our lives in constant fear, as this fear quickly turns into hypervigilance and panic. When we have a great deal of stress in our lives, we overprocess the stress response, and the chemicals that this produces in our bodies are very harmful. Living in constant stress or fear for significant periods can result in post-traumatic stress disorder, or PTSD. This is the ego-based life: if you live your life solely based on instinct, you will be surviving at best, without the ability to rest, and your body will eventually turn against itself with sickness and disease. Perhaps you know people who are living like this.

Indeed, some people live in fear and become victims, and there are also people who live in fear—a thought process more than an emotion. Think of someone who may be living on a power trip, focusing on how they can control their partners, children, and employees/coworkers: often, when someone feels out of control within, they turn to controlling the people around them, while some people are so overwhelmed with life and their responsibilities that they seek a way to numb their self-talk and quiet their mind. The constant chatter and negativity in their head become disabling, and as a coping mechanism, they may turn to alcohol, drugs, narcotics, or even sex to find momentary relief from their thoughts. This, however, is only a temporary fix, and more and more of the chosen substance will slowly be required to prolong the same level of numbness.

There is a better way than this: instead of focusing on your base instincts and numbing your senses, God can guide you and offer you peace of mind. God's peace is beyond understanding. It's been my experience that when life is crazy and out of control, if you seek God, He will still your mind, holding you in His spiritual realm, where you will find joy and peace. This is powerful, and this is God's Light shining through you. In this way, the people who are watching you will wonder how you handle the circumstances in your life.

It was God's Holy Spirit within me that allowed me to find rest in my journey, forgive the injustices I had been faced with, and discover lessons along the way through my own self-reflection. I was able, through the power of the Spirit, to become stronger with a firm yet gentle response. His power flowed through me. People in my life witnessed me grow and change while enduring massive pressure and conflict. I was told that my countenance had changed, too, and that it was clear something significant was happening in my life.

People tell me that I am a trendsetter and that my courageous spirit manifests in the form of me being a thought leader. I believe, however, that this is not me that they are seeing, but God's love, peace, and guiding light. Remember this: Without God, we are merely the self-absorbed ego. Hence, we must remember to point others to God and to share the light He has placed within us. The world is a dark place and is only getting darker daily, so we need as much light as we can get!

There is an abundance of pain in the world, and neither you nor I can fix all the pain. What we *can* do is focus on serving the ones brought to us. The world's pain is addressed one soul at a time; there is no mass "fix". Well, Jesus is the mass fix, and He is brought into the hearts of individuals one person at a time.

While working in a higher management role in corporate America, I found myself directing a lot more time and energy to the demands of my career. In 2008, after granting the father of my youngest two children and his new wife a two-week vacation with my children, they filed a hearing, accusing me of abusing my then-eleven-year-old daughter, their underlying intention being to have my children live with them full-time.

My life and identity as a mother were immediately thrown into crisis at this time. This was when I decided to take time off from my rapidly progressing career to regroup and focus full-time on my values and priorities: my faith, my children, and my growth.
My grief was overbearing. I experienced how emotional grief and pain, when turned inward, attack the physical body. My emotional grief was so great that my hips literally went out of alignment and I could barely walk.

After that twelve-month work sabbatical, I re-entered the workforce in higher education as a subject matter expert (rather than a manager or director) to keep myself productive and distract myself from the ongoing custody battle. While I wanted my primary focus where it belonged (i.e., on my family), I needed to have my energy focused elsewhere for a better balance. The custody case was taking much longer than I had expected, and because energy attracts like energy, it felt like my life was becoming a constant crisis.

After working in the university for a year, departments merged, and I found myself moving from working under a compassionate boss to working under a bully—a boss that appeared to be hellbent on ruining lives. Most of the employees in the thirty-five-person team left to get away from his abuse, including my prior boss. There were, however, a few of us who, due to life circumstances, decided we would stick it out. After all, bosses come and go, right?

Lesson learned: Whenever possible, remove yourself from poor leadership—especially when that comes in the form of an abusive, bullying leader. Similarly, do not be loyal to a company: the company will keep moving, and you can always return to the company if management turns over. To stay in a position under poor leadership will certainly take its toll on your self-esteem, and may ruin or set back your career. This will surely harm your personal and family life, as well. It's true what they say: People don't leave bad jobs; they leave bad bosses.

The silver lining for me now as a leadership consultant is that I compassionately understand and can identify with what a troubled work environment looks and feels like: I know firsthand the devastation that a bullying boss has on the lives of employees and the damage it does to the company. Hence, if you'd like to take a short workplace assessment to determine if your work environment is toxic, my free PDF *3 Christian Values That Will Increase Your Profit$* would be perfect for you. It includes a workplace assessment and is available for download at go.candacemae.com.

It's honestly a wonder why I stayed in that toxic environment: I knew the importance of being in an environment that was conducive to growth, yet I felt there was too much to deal with in my life for me to start in a new role with a new company, since this would require me to put my best foot forward—something I felt unable to do at the time. On top of the ongoing custody case and three years of co-parenting challenges, courses, counseling sessions, and court appearances, my then-twelve-year-old son was diagnosed with a seventy percent scoliosis curvature in his spine that required a five-hour surgery to implant two sixteen-inch stainless steel rods along his spine. My youngest daughter, then fourteen, was also experiencing some mental health challenges and suicidal ideations at the time, and my then-husband had additionally offended my oldest daughter (whom he adopted as an adult), so I was dealing with the strains of their relationship, too, and the ripple effects that created: three years with no contact with my oldest daughter and grandchildren!

My husband at that time was an executive at a worldwide company, and his income was more than we needed, so I mentioned staying home to get out of the toxic work environment. My husband did not want me to stop working, however—probably because he was concerned I would be emotionally engulfed by our children-related challenges if I didn't have work as an outlet. He encouraged me to keep working, do my best, and prove to Human Resources that my boss was a bully. He had full faith in my ability to provide the evidence needed to stop my boss and find resolve for myself and my team. I knew I could do it, too, but it would require a sacrifice of my energy. But then again, what were the alternatives?

Life's circumstances became unbearable for a few years. As I look back, I am in awe that I even made it through! This is something I would not have been able to do without my faith: with it, I focused on staying positive, finding ways to grow my leadership and faith. I found solace in home decorating, yard work, and spending what time I could with my husband. These things made me happy. For much of my time outside of work, I was fully engaged in preparing court documents and documenting interactions with the children's father, as well as observations of the children when with us. The stark and swift changes in my daughter's behavior were blatant, and all of this had to be meticulously documented for the courts.

My energy was so focused on the chaos of the alienation/custody case, my children's health issues, and my hostile work environment (energy draws like energy) that there seemed to be no light at the end of the tunnel.

Nonetheless, I enjoyed what time I had with my children, and was determined to be the sunshine and cheerleader at work despite my boss. Hence, I put tools in place to keep my spirits high (e.g., daily inspirational videos that I would forward to teammates), and I developed strong relationships outside our department, seeking ambassadorship and training opportunities that would allow me to volunteer my time and put distance between me and my boss, with the bonus of keeping my skills sharp in the areas that I enjoyed, especially since my boss was limiting my power and contributions within the department. I put as much energy as I could into positive growth, despite the circumstances.

I was able to document the interactions of the bullying boss, although it was a long journey: it would be two years before something was done. I trusted the administration team at the beginning, walking through the chain of command to address injustices and poorly written job performances that were blatantly distorted. I was told by the leading administrator in our division who oversaw the initial Human Resources concerns that he was addressing my concerns, only to find out he was not; he was tying up my time so that the allotted time to file a complaint with official Human Resources department expired, repeatedly.

I also discovered through my filing of a grievance with the central Human Resources department that they didn't want anyone to share witnessed behavior on behalf of other employees, so I could only address matters that concerned me, rather than present ongoing patterns substantiated by other employees. Furthermore, the position I served in was not represented by a union, so my colleagues and I had no additional representation.

Regardless of these issues, I continued to document events—so that in the second year, when my performance review mentioned something that had happened the year before (which brought it back up to a "current issue" that could be addressed), I was able to file an official complaint with the central Human Resources department and provide all the documentation showing the evidence of the bullying I had endured. Here, I was able to bring enlightenment to central HR and recommend the use of a 360-degree leadership assessment with leaders, which provides anonymous feedback from all levels of a leader's sphere of influence, revealing how others experience them and highlighting any blind spots and professional growth areas. This enables the development of personalized professional development work, and is also where executive coaching can be instrumental, since it can pinpoint any limiting beliefs that are currently negatively impacting leadership (and remember, strengthening leadership skills increases productivity and reduces company liability!). If you or an organization you know could benefit from the use of a 360-degree leadership assessment, one is available on my website (https://candacemae.com/assessments).

It was a loaded complaint with lots of concrete, tangible examples. I had to cite policies that had been broken, not just describe the inappropriate leadership behavior. Poor behavior alone would not be addressed; without citing a policy, the complaint was invalid. I also had to make recommendations regarding how the behavior could be corrected, which was a simple task for me, considering I was preparing to be a leadership coach!

I am happy to share that the poor leadership matter was addressed: my recommendations were put into place and the bullying director eventually left the university, although not the system; he was moved into a position in which he managed systems rather than people. The damage from that boss had already devasted the lives of many colleagues, however: I watched personalities that were highly engaged and bright become thwarted and shut down, leading to some leaving the university prematurely.

The lesson here is that keeping your integrity, self-confidence, and self-esteem when being interrogated and slammed for years on end is a tough road to endure. Do bear in mind that I was working within this toxic work environment at the same time that I was dealing with an alienation/custody court case, which featured years of attacks, documenting, and proving inaccuracies. Exhausting!

Choose your battles. You can easily document your life away and go through life surviving rather than thriving, but no job is worth that! Had it not been for my faith and tenacity, I am not sure how I would have made it through. My husband notably didn't: he grew angry and bitter because he was unable to protect me and my children from the broken family court system—yet another broken systemic issue. It was too difficult for him to watch our lives be ripped apart. I chose not to walk away from my children, but to stand and fight on their behalf.

We all have choices regarding how we react or respond. If you repress anger and injustice, it will eat at your health and view of the world. I'm a strong advocate of the idea that we each do our work, find our voice, and speak our truth. Be the change you want to see in the world, model positive behavior in all circumstances, and let others catch your enthusiasm.

As I write this, I now see a pattern that has run through my life: there seems to have always been a bully throughout the entirety of my life. I have always been standing up to bullies to prove that they don't control me. Indeed, I was also a witness to systemic bullying at a young age—but more on this later!

I became a certified trainer for Operational Excellence, a grassroots program across the campus to change the culture. I had already gotten certified as a diversity trainer and led several workshops, the follow-up surveys of which reporting that I was engaging and high-energy and that my participants ultimately felt moved and ready to act. Yet at one workshop, I noticed my leadership was thwarted, and I felt unable to shake it. Two admin staff from the division I worked in were in attendance, and these individuals were bullies towards staff and student workers, having inflicted harm upon several people in the division. This made me apprehensive of their intentions for attending.

Note that what you focus on expands.

I began to feel constricted by their presence, and I was unable to let my energy flow freely; not until I heard one of them ask, "What if you're asked to do something from the boss above you that you don't agree with?" Suddenly, I felt there was hope for them: perhaps rather than intentionally being bullies, their abusive and manipulative behaviors toward staff were the result of them essentially acting as puppets, carrying out evil tasks as ordered and not realizing they have a choice in how they respond to inappropriate requests from supervisors and how they handle things. After all, I had been in that position myself years earlier, so my compassion immediately went out to them. There was suddenly no longer a sense of threat; rather, I felt my energy and enthusiasm to create positive organizational change kick in. I became fully engaged in leading the workshop.

It is interesting to see how our body's defenses automatically kick in to protect us from perceived threats. It's also interesting (as noted by Wayne Dyer) that when we change the way we look at things, the things we look at change.

I spoke with the Head of Human Resources after the workshop and explained what I thought was happening, and asked if my behavior while leading the workshop had changed upon my drawing this conclusion. She said there had been a noticeable difference in my energy at the beginning and that it was evident when I finally broke free into my full energetic presence. I hadn't been able to control my fearful reaction: my body had been functioning in response to fear.

Today, ten years later, I have built enough capacity within myself where hopefully if put in that same situation, I would have enough consciousness to exhibit a response that would override the fear I felt at the beginning.

As you reflect on *your* soul's journey, look for repetition and patterns. Unconscious beliefs get passed down from generation to generation, and you must break these corrupt patterns after becoming aware of these generational issues. Educate your family about them. Do not be afraid, for God is with you. God has called us not to be timid, but to be bold in our faith and actions.

Most people are locked in shame; in the dark: they want to live a healthy life, but they do not know how. They may not even see the patterns within themselves, as these are ingrained in them as "normal", yet in reality, these beliefs actually create unconscious assumptions that limit what opportunities we see as being before us. People consistently miss opportunities that are obvious to others because of their limited level of awareness.

So, how do we go about increasing our awareness and the awareness of others? Ask key questions. That will penetrate hearts. Create an awareness of the pain. For many years, I was not aware of all the pain in the world, let alone my own pain—and then when I *did* see pain, I was only aware of my *own* pain. I did not see pain in others in the world, yet I've discovered since that everyone has pain, and their pain is real. Each of us must become aware of our own pain. In observing my daughter and her cousins, I see the common challenges they share, even though they didn't grow up together. I also see patterns in my adopted nieces and nephews—patterns likely passed onto them environmentally, since they were adopted at such young ages.

Do you see the patterns of pain in your life? What about those of the people close to you? It's quite common that the pain that was in our lives at some point or another will show up again in the lives of our grown children. I believe this presents an opportunity for us to see such unresolved pain and embrace it.

Help your family to see their own pain and the patterns within that stem from the generational thoughts and beliefs that are passed down. Awareness and observation are the first steps required for growth.

If you're wondering how to go about developing a stronger sense of awareness, I offer holistic coaching geared for leaders that embraces all areas of life: the physical, emotional, intellectual, spiritual, and energetic. What happens in one area of life crosses over into all areas of life and directly impacts our careers and businesses. If you're interested in meeting to discuss your situation, I offer a free consultation, which I have opened up to you, as a reader of this book. You can book in through my online calendar (available at https://candacemae.com/schedule-an-appointment).

CHAPTER 4:
SYSTEMIC ISSUES

S O, WHERE DOES THE TRUE danger of these pain patterns lie? The answer to this is *when it affects those in power,* since this naturally leads to systemic challenges and pain in organizations, too. The world reflects human generational pain within organizations, and this evolves into systemic patterns that run throughout society and permeate organizations, communities, and the world as a whole. People have intrinsic value, yet as a society, we tend to slap labels on people to put them in a box, in turn limiting their worth—when in actuality, people are multifaceted and it's the uniqueness of everyone that makes life interesting and powerful. This means leaders in companies and organizations need to understand the principles and patterns that sustain such systemic issues so they can break free of such constraints.

The world today is at a tipping point. Consider all these events that have come into focus while the world was essentially shut down and people were mandated to stay at home unless they were an essential worker during COVID, in turn bringing the entire world into hyper-vigilance:

- The United States establishing a mandatory stay-at-home order in March 2020, starting on March 11, with an order blocking the assembly of over two hundred and fifty people. On March 17 (St. Patrick's Day), this was restricted to less than ten people per gathering. Bars, restaurants, businesses, and even churches were all shut down, resulting in a large push for online church sessions and virtual meetings.

- The political unrest and polarization in the United States, with added pressure due to it being a presidential election year.

- The video of George Floyd, an American black man who died from a police officer pressing his knee into his neck for over eight minutes while handcuffed, the footage of whose death on May 25 went viral, spurring riots internationally.

- The deep conversations being held on social media and in personal lives concerning understanding the term "white privilege". White privilege is defined as the "inherent advantages possessed by a white person on the basis of their race in a society characterized by racial inequality and injustice". It concerns being able to walk into a store and find that the main displays of shampoo are catered to your hair type and skin tone; it is being able to turn on the television and see people of your race widely represented; it is being able to move through life without being racially profiled or unfairly stereotyped.

- The waves of new posts on social media about the "Me Too" movement, a social movement started by Tarana Burke in

2006 advocating for female survivors of sexual violence to speak out about their experiences.

- The voices of the other groups who wanted to be heard and remembered for the injustices done to them, such as Anti-Semitism (i.e., hostility toward or discrimination against Jews as a religious, ethnic, or racial group).
- The heightened focus on the homeless in the United States, since it became critical to get them off the streets during COVID.
- The international installation of 5G Internet while everyone was home, oblivious. 5G technology will change how we interact with the world overnight: now, automation is fully functioning at a global level and is ready to be rolled out ubiquitously, which will drastically change the dynamics of the world and increase the wealth-to-poverty gap.
- The shutting down of the personal profile accounts of world leaders' who chose to have controversial discissions about COVID-19, 5G Internet, and other big topics on Facebook, YouTube, and LinkedIn without notification. This was a massive red flag regarding freedom of speech being restricted.

All these events (and more) combined to create a perfect storm of unrest and pushed a high focus on the Civil Rights Movement.

Some examples of societal and systemic issues may be seen best in the interactions and behaviors of the political world in which our government and businesses function. People do what people see, and what is our government and are our politicians modeling in leadership? Hatred, manipulation, and twisted truths. As you look around (especially during election years), you may notice that those running for office spend more time focusing on slandering and highlighting what the *other* party and candidates are doing and/or not doing or how the *other* party and candidates will destroy our country with more vim and vigor than they spend sharing what their own views are, backed by tangible strategies they propose to put in place. It's as if they believe bashing the reputations of others will somehow lift them to a higher stature.

We witness this same destructive behavior in many workplaces, too: people do what people see.

To lead from this, there is still a stronghold of control and dominance in business that ripples through the sense of worthiness felt in employees. Rather than embracing people for the intrinsic value they have and seeking to leverage and enhance their strengths so they can be better associates or employees and feel encouraged to share their insights and creativity in the workplace, many in key management roles focus on highlighting the flaws and growth areas of employees, thus reducing their confidence and devaluing what they can contribute. How often have you seen managers label employees by their weaknesses, rather than by their strengths? It's truly a matter of perspective.

Rather than pitting people against each other, we need to focus on the common ground we share and celebrate the differences of perspective with civility and respect. Rather than judging, labeling, segregating, and isolating people, we would do better to look at their core issues and instead seek healing, integration, and growth.

Indeed, it is because many people struggle with how to heal, integrate, and grow that my complementary introductory workshop on how to communicate using connection, rather than merely transactional conversations that only exchange information, trains leaders and their teams on how to:

- Connect.
- Find the strengths in their associates and team members.
- Leverage those strengths.

- Coach others for growth.
- Integrate actionable values into their workplace culture.
- Lead by example, where values penetrate policy and procedure in daily operations and life.

...And so much more.

Building your business through building your workers has a ripple effect that not only creates a positive organizational impact, but also increases your business on all levels—and not only this, but it also builds the skills of the people who will ultimately go home and create positive impact for their families and communities.

You may believe technology is the best way to build your business, and while it certainly has its place, technology is only as good as the people who engage with it. As a business leader, you have a great opportunity and responsibility to lead with love, invest in the growth of your team, and subsequently change lives and positively impact the world.

It is my goal to create awareness and movement concerning how and why to lead with love for greater impact. I develop leadership that CARES through Communication, Attitude, Relationships and Retention, Equipping teams with emotional intelligence, and Sales. I provide a wealth of additional information on my website (www.candacemae.com).

Let's now look at health and some of the systemic issues that surround this topic. As multifaceted individuals, we have physical, mental, emotional, and spiritual health—and yet rather than embracing our health holistically, western society segments these areas. If someone has a physical health issue *that we can observe*, we tend to be more compassionate and accommodating towards their needs; however, when it comes to those with *invisible* disabilities, we tend to minimize and shame them for seeking help. While the USA has laws to bring awareness to the needs of the disabled under the Americans with Disabilities Act, such laws alone do not enforce compliance; rather, change comes when individuals take responsibility for doing what is right and embrace others for their intrinsic value. Compliance with a law is more superficial, as it is done for the sole purpose of avoiding a financial penalty. Worse yet, some individuals actively seek out organizations in violation of those laws to bring about lawsuits for personal gain.

Often, enforcement through law only creates the outward appearances of compliance; how people are embraced with regards to sharing their insights and perspectives within the organizations themselves is an entirely different dialogue. Sure, there are cutting-edge companies that have high values and are beginning to model integration and collaboration and place employees in strength-focused positions, yet these are still ridiculously small in number—and this must change. It's a proven fact that when training is reinforced with coaching, eighty percent of the changed behavior gets retained, as in this way, the principles are put into action.

Other systemic issues revolve around mental health and the stigmas associated with the labels given, as well as spiritual topics and judging individuals based on religion. In general, the mass population is angry and thus lashes out when it comes to discussing differences, rather than calmly and respectfully debating and engaging in a deeper conversation to understand (and even celebrate) their differences of opinion. As a result of both the COVID-19 pandemic and the Civil Rights Movement for Black Lives Matter around the world, however, more and more people have begun to open up to the prospect of having difficult discussions and listening to different perspectives. Even so, there has been massive rioting, since people are angry and refuse to engage in healthy dialogue, instead turning to violence to express their frustrations.

As individuals become aware of the depth of the human plight (i.e., the systemic issues that I've been referring to), they realize the importance of their choices. It was our ancestors choice to disobey God that created the fallen state of this world we now live in.

It's time to make choices for the good of ourselves and our society as a whole. The civil protests and riots stemming from years of pent-up rage over police brutality were triggered by the recorded death of George Floyd that we mentioned earlier. Even while George begged to be released, stating he could not breathe, and fellow civilians stood there shouting for the officers to release him, the officers continued pressure for two minutes after George passed out.

Of course, this horrific act being captured on video by various bystanders from various angles is one of many examples in recent history showing that we need to turn the tide. This video went viral on the Internet, bringing attention to the heartbreaking act and proving once again that black lives are being threatened—and not as a one-off incident or out of self-defense.

We must be the voice to bring awareness to family members, coworkers, and communities throughout the world; we must hold each other accountable, rather than turning our heads in ignorance. One person at a time is how we make change. Each team and organization is only as strong as its weakest link, and the ultimate work within such organizations begins with everyone (*each one*) owning their thoughts and behaviors.

Many white people initially struggled to understand the phrase "Black Lives Matter"; we would respond with, "*All* lives matter," which would infuriate the black population, as it indicated to them that we did not understand their pain or the challenges they were facing. Clearly, we did not understand the magnitude and blatancy of the problem that was the murdering of black men on the streets of the

USA, usually by the hands of police officers—the very people we are to call upon for assistance when in danger.

Telling their stories is the only way to bring attention to the matter, and though the stories may be watered down by the media and painted as one-off situations or the result of a police officer acting in self-defense, the black community continues to tell its stories across the United States, sometimes capturing these on video and sharing them over the Internet to bring global awareness.

To add fuel to the fire, the George Floyd incident occurred during COVID, when everyone was glued to their phones, the Internet, and television. This formed the perfect storm: riots began happening across the United States in response to the incident. Riots are the voices of the unheard, and it was through these riots that even more awareness was brought to the matter—and now, discussions around how to change are abundant.

It's my hope that you can find some answers here concerning how to make this change yourself; that my stories will resonate with you, bring awareness to your own experiences, and invite you to self-reflect. Systemic changes are not corrected by the passing of new laws alone; systemic change happens at an individual level, requiring each person to pause, look in the mirror, and examine what they are doing and how they are behaving. What are you thinking? What are the unconscious beliefs and assumptions you hold that impact your day-to-day actions?

I myself experienced one poignant example of the side-effects such systemic oppression can cause: during college, I accepted an accounting intern position at a local hospital alongside a male colleague. The administrative nurse treated me very poorly, yet was exceedingly kind to my male colleague. The nurse would go on rants, call me names, and give me demeaning jobs that did not use any of my skills, and it was clear from her rants that she did not like me because of my red hair and first name. She was singling me out, treating me horrifically, and blatantly blaming me for things I did not do. My male counterpart even spoke up several times, stating, "Candace did not do that." However, she would ignore him and continue to admonish me. My fellow colleague watched in disdain, and after maybe a week, he said, "Candace, we're quitting this job. It is not acceptable for her to treat you this way—not even if you *did* do something wrong."

As it turns out in this situation, the administrative nurse was a black woman striking out against me because she knew another white girl with red hair who had the same name, and she didn't like something that girl had done to her—so I was being punished as a result. My colleague's values, however, were so strong that he spoke out about the poor leadership behavior, and when nothing changed, he said, "This is not an environment I am willing to work in, and you're not staying here either, Candace!" Well, good for him! He understood the value and importance of working in a healthy environment and he valued me, and even though he knew I was a single mom who needed the money, he made sure I did not stay in such a toxic environment. My classmate and colleague had stronger boundaries, self-respect and convictions than I did at that time.

The lesson here? We all have choices to make concerning what we will tolerate, how we ourselves will behave, and what treatment we are willing to accept from others. What are *your* actions creating? People project their issues onto and act out towards others based on their own experiences and filters. Hence, it is important that we have boundaries and that we respect ourselves (and others) enough to be willing to draw a line in the sand regarding how we and the people around us are treated. We must be willing to speak up when we see other people being mistreated, which may require a sacrifice on our part: my colleague was well-liked and being treated well, yet he valued my treatment, and quit this job to make a point of principle.

I am a natural advocate for others. After all, my communication style is that of an "advocate": I have natural strengths of protection and a tendency to challenge the status quo. My desire is always to create positive organizational change through empowered associates and compassionate leaders.

Perhaps you've had similar experiences in the workplace. If this is the case, be gentle with yourself! Take care of yourself first and then consider seeking work with another organization—or start one of your own, where you can create your own positive culture! This starts with you. Don't become bitter; become better! It's not what life does to you that counts; it's how you respond to it.

Similarly, my ex-husband despised the behavior of the senior management at a previous company he worked at—and yet this very same behavior that he claimed to despise he incorporated and emulated as he became a part of senior management at another company. Was it peer pressure? No, it was more than that: we are designed to subconsciously bring to fruition that which our energy focuses on. On top of this, our subconscious doesn't recognize negatives, so when we say, "I will never do such and such," our subconscious only hears, "I will do such and such." Our internal mechanism recreates those very things we are suppressing and want to avoid!

Stop a moment to reflect on your life. Do you see a pattern of things you said you would never do somehow creeping into fruition in your life? This often manifests in subtle ways: a woman who was molested at a young age may find that her thoughts during sex involve reliving those horrific experiences, and she has no idea why, for example. She may not even recognize this until it is brought to her attention, and this experience will bring about shame and reduced self-confidence, even without her realizing it is happening.

A life unexamined is a life full of repeated patterns. Trapped emotions will create patterns of behavior. Have you noticed the same emotional states repeating in different relationships? We retraumatize ourselves without consciously realizing that is what we are doing, and this is the result of unconscious beliefs ruling our behavior patterns.

These patterns will also often span multiple generations. Why? Because from conception through to our being seven years of age, we are sponges absorbing all the events around us, forming "truths" or "programs" in our unconscious minds. Here, we are picking up the beliefs and behaviors of our parents, family, and environment, meaning that we also pick up the false beliefs upheld in previous generations. You can, however, be thankful for all the things in life that trigger a negative feeling inside of you, because that negative feeling is a warning—a gift—telling you that something is out of alignment with your divine nature. Here, you are being given an opportunity to examine your thoughts and beliefs and hold them up to God's Truth to see what is out of alignment. This is how we discover what false beliefs we have that control us. Imagine if you realized this earlier in life! Socrates was right when he said, "The unexamined life is not worth living." The person with an unexamined life is simply not living freely, but is controlled by their hidden beliefs *without knowing it*. They are living in a trance-like state or on autopilot mode, thinking life is happening *to* them rather than *through* them; that the outcome of their life is a matter of Fate. They think they must live the cards they were dealt, with no options for change. This happens when we are disconnected from God; when we don't have the Spirit guiding us. Can you see why God warned that by having the knowledge of good and evil without a connection to God's Spirit, we would be dead?

Our minds and bodies are incredibly powerful: we only consciously use about five percent of our mind, while the other ninety-five percent runs in a trance-like state or on autopilot based on the habits we've formed through the repetition of behavior, controlled by the unconscious mind.

The lesson we can take from this? We must take an inventory of the events in our lives and acknowledge and embrace the good, the bad, and the indifference in our lives, rather than living in denial or resisting what is there. When we are in a relationship with Christ, His Spirit guides us through this transformation. Without His Spirit, it is much more difficult to undergo this transformation, and we will never have the assurance of an abundant, eternal spiritual life. Notably, the complementary PDF, *The You Factor: Finding Your Unique Gift Mix*, will walk you through this self-inventory process. Visit https://giftmix.candacemae.com to download your copy.

CHAPTER 5:
THE PURPOSE OF EMOTION

HOW DO WE COME TO live in denial or in a state in which we resist what's happened to us?

When we are in the process of repressing our feelings, we stop breathing during difficult conversations and experiences (a sign that we are numbing and trapping emotions); when we don't like what has or is happening to us, we create this state of resistance and denial. When we resist admitting what emotion we are feeling, that feeling doesn't go away, however: it gets trapped in our physical body and cumulates there, leaving us with bodily pain—a signal that we have undealt-with emotion that is hurting us. The bad feelings do not simply go away; instead, they continue until we embrace them. What we resist persists!

Everything is energy. Our true self is energy, and our thoughts, words, and bodies are energy. Lower levels of energy form matter, and in this physical realm (the earth), we have lower levels of energy and gravity that hold this matter in place. Emotion is energy-in-motion (e-motion) and is a gift to us to be used as a guidance system for our lives: when we feel joy, we are in alignment; when we feel pain or fear, this is a signal that something is not in alignment. Embracing our understanding of emotion this way is extremely helpful.

If we could be like a baby and let our emotions roll through us like a wave, it would be much easier to stay in a positive, higher frequency of life. Notice the fact that children have a natural resilience when it comes to bouncing back, yet through conditioning and negative feedback from our environment, we are taught to deny, suppress, or repress our emotions.

I've recently come to understand that emotions are sensations we feel in our bodies—a *huge* awareness. Many of us stay busy so we don't feel too much and thus have a hard time with slowing down, since when we do, we suddenly have an overwhelming sense of anxiety in our bodies that we don't know how to process. Many are also afraid of the uncomfortable sensations or pain that they avoid feeling through busyness or other distractions, whether they be substances, sexual, working excessively, etc. When we avoid emotional pain, however, that discomfort gets trapped in our bodies and creates dis-ease.

So, how do you deal with and release these emotions?

There are several ways of releasing trapped emotions, but first, it's worth noting that when we sit still for a few minutes, we become aware of a lot of various sensations in our bodies that we don't notice when we're busy rushing around. This is our emotions showing up as sensations in our bodies. I wish I'd known this at an earlier age. Stop and think about this:

- What does joy feel like? Have you ever been so excited and happy that you could hardly contain yourself? Here, your body—every cell—experiences an uplifting sensation. When I'm elated and full of joy, I want to jump, spin, run, and shout with joy!
- What does anger feel like? Hot. We often hear anger described as "blood boiling".

Become aware of what sensations your body elicits for each emotion and then allow yourself to become aware of those sensations throughout the day (and embrace those feelings as time permits). This is key to releasing emotions. Carving out time in your day to sit in meditation and allow the busyness of your thoughts to clear and to just feel and be in the present moment is extremely powerful and allows your body to heal.

Some emotions that have created pain are trapped in your body, so when you initially sit still and begin to feel the sensations, focus your attention on the pain, sending love and breath to the pain area. The pain may intensify at first, but don't be afraid: remind yourself, *I am safe to feel; I am safe in my body.* After a couple of minutes, the pain will disperse, and you'll feel peace.

When dealing with more traumatic feelings, it's extremely helpful to have someone with you to guide you through the process and remind you that you're safe. What's important is that you feel the sensations and identify and embrace the feeling (whether that be sadness, grief, anger—whatever it is), but not go into the *story* that caused the feeling. You will experience images and memories associated with that pain flashing up. That's an emotion you're tapping into! It's critical that you do not go into reliving these details of the story; rather, keep your thoughts (your mind) out of the feeling and just allow your body to feel the sensations of anger, sadness, grief, betrayal, etc. Again, the pain in your body may increase, but just when you think you can't stand the pain anymore, it will begin to release, and a gentle quiet and stillness will come over you. You will find relief in this way; it's the Law of Transmutation.

Transmutation is defined as the action of changing or the state of being changed into another form. In this context, the negative emotions are vibrating at a lower frequency (remember that everything is energy, and emotions are energy-in-motion, with each emotion possessing its own vibrational frequency). Negative emotions have a lower frequency and positive emotions have a higher frequency, so when we sit with lower emotions and allow our bodies to feel those sensations (or vibrations), the trapped energy starts to unwind and move out of the cells they were trapped in, being transformed or transmuted into a higher energy frequency.

When we do not allow ourselves to embrace those lower emotions, they get trapped in the cells of our bodies and accumulate over time, leading to disease (dis-ease) in our bodies. This makes us sick.

Your body will heal itself if you become aware of how your body was designed and how it functions. This is counterintuitive in western civilization: instead of following ancient wisdom, western medicine wants to provide manmade medicines and surgeries to numb the pain and cut out body parts—and while this succeeds in treating the symptoms, it does not address the core issues.

Not only is what I'm sharing with you scientifically proven, but I myself have lived through this experience of transmuting locked emotions in my body. I have had PTSD and lived through multiple traumatic experiences, the associated emotions of which I did not process for many years, leaving them trapped in my body. I spent over forty years in personal growth, seeking wholeness, and though I have experienced massive growth, I was still plagued with a sense of being "stuck"; a sense that something was wrong with me. Something was not in alignment, yet all my coaches and mentors told me I was doing everything right. Then, one day, near the end of a year-long business mastery program where I shared pieces of my story throughout the year, a beautiful soul contacted me and asked if I was open to receiving help from her. She was hesitant to reach out but felt a strong intuition telling her to.

I am so grateful that she did: she was an answer to a prayer! She was able to walk me through this transmutation process, getting in touch with the emotions trapped in my body and facilitating them being transmuted, in turn allowing me to become aware of the deep-seated beliefs that stemmed all the way back to me being four years of age. Those beliefs stemmed from the traumatic experiences I had then, but they no longer serve me now; in fact, I call those beliefs "false beliefs". Many of those false beliefs stirred up fear. Fear can be described as False Evidence Appearing Real (FEAR).

So, sit with the emotional pain in your body for at least two minutes and just let the emotion have its way with you. You may cry and you may start to shake, and that's okay; just let the energy have its way with you and *feel* so it can be flushed from its trapped holdings in our body. Let that negative energy be released and turned into a higher frequency of energy.

I worked through a series of nine weekly meetings to work through this process, as I found I had many layers of emotional pain to deal with. Our sessions were approximately two hours long each, and it took about twenty minutes each time for me to be able to tap into my feelings seriously; I was so wrapped up in my thoughts and intellect, keeping myself so busy with racing thoughts, that I could not tap into feelings.

This was when I discovered that emotions have bodily sensations. My therapist would ask me to get in touch with an emotion or a bodily sensation, and although I couldn't tap into my feelings, I could identify shooting pains or an awareness of a bodily pain I previously hadn't noticed. Then, she'd ask me, "What's the feeling or thought that comes there?" I would immediately start to tell a story or talk in-depth, and she would stop me and say, "Brief answers." Then, I would begin to slow my mind, and there would be a flood of images and memories that would come—and *then* I could find the feeling. It was important that I didn't go into the stories; that I felt the emotion only. I would spend around two hours during the first few sessions shaking, and sometimes deep crying would also come.

I was thrilled to experience this release: afterwards, I felt elation and joy where previously there had been sadness and grief. You see, when we are in the present moment, joy, goodwill, and gratitude are our core emotions. Once we embrace and transform the emotion we embody, we become free to move into higher states of thought and experience transformed behavior. Remember, everything we experience is filtered through the beliefs held in our unconscious, so until we make the unconscious conscious, we will be controlled and think it is simply our Fate at play. This is essential to keep at the forefront of our daily awareness: think about what you are thinking about! Capture your thoughts and examine them to see what is true, what is no longer serving you, and what is holding you back. The easiest way to do this is through an intentional meditation exercise, which I have included in your companion booklet. Refer to this and complete the exercise in the corresponding chapter.

By sitting still and feeling emotion without allowing your mind to relive the details of the associated story, instead merely experiencing the feelings and bodily sensations that come about, healing occurs. The pain in the body is where the emotion is stored, and while this pain may grow stronger as we embrace these feelings and sensations, it will only last for about two minutes before it begins to dissipate.

Staying grounded inside your body may be difficult during those two minutes, but if you can remind yourself that you are safe and can fully embrace your emotions and pain during those two minutes (or until it subsides), the pain will disintegrate and be gone for good.

Caution: Do not do this alone to start. Instead, it's best to initially have someone walk you through this so you're not alone and so they can check in with you and be sure you're not getting into the details of the story, which could cause negative results. Having someone guide you through this process will enable them to remind you that you're safe in the moment.

Once, I was sitting "in the feeling" during therapy, when suddenly, my entire body reacted: my arms pulled up to my chest and my upper torso twisted to the right as I was sitting. My body wanted to stand up and start running! My guide (therapist) was observing me (as I sat with my eyes closed) and, upon noticing this, she reminded me that I was safe in my body and to not resist, but to let the energy have its way with me. That's how our bodies protect us: they don't want us to feel that sadness or grief again, so they attempt to repress or flee from the pain.

Completing a meditation practice daily is a positive coping mechanism that can serve us in many positive ways. Meditation builds the capacity for us to hold more energy and space for ourselves and others, and in this way, we become able to sit quietly for longer periods. It also strengthens one's ability to focus and be calmer.

It also builds one's capacity to use their imagination—a powerful thing, as it is possible to essentially use your imagination to create future memories of your ideal life. Envisioning the future with detail as if it were happening today enables one's internal subconscious mechanism to work in their favor to bring about the behavior needed for them to *be* the person they desire; their imagined state. You see, our subconscious doesn't know the difference between what is real and what is imagined, and when we understand this, the doors of possibility open to us.

It may be easier for you to understand this when you think about today's technology: through gaming and 3D/4D experiences, we feel as though we are truly experiencing something that is, in actuality, only a computer game—so if your mind doesn't know the difference between what is physically happening and what is imagined through computer imagery, think about the power of envisioning your ideal future and feeling it with all of your senses as if it were actually happening right this second! Indeed, if this exercise is done enough times, we can program our subconscious mind to make this our reality—which will then do everything in its power to draw those experiences to us. Accordingly, we will develop habits that align with our ideal selves.

Our self-talk is another powerful tool. Start paying attention to what you're thinking and what the voices inside your head are saying. We all have an ongoing conversation in our minds called self-talk, and it's now your job to make sure that it's positive self-talk!

As we build our capacity to focus through the practice of meditation, our listening ability also strengthens, meaning we can more easily focus on the communication techniques someone is using to hear beyond what they are saying with their words. Put differently, we can learn to listen to what is not being said. After all, words only form seven percent of the message; thirty-eight percent of the message is the tone, pitch, and tempo in which the message is delivered, while the other fifty-five percent is body language, posture, facial expressions, breathing patterns, and whether we're matching or mirroring the speaker in terms of body position. With practice, we can focus our attention on the speaker long enough to hear the meaning behind their words, understand their intent, and hear what they are *not* saying!

Learning to listen and communicate effectively is pivotal when it comes to solving the relationship struggles that are familiar to many of us. It was recently, during the early months of COVID, that I got the opportunity to spend time with my second daughter and walk through this process of understanding our differing perspectives. My daughter was hurting deeply with severe emotional pain and was struggling with depression and suicidal thoughts. Mental health issues and grief over the death of her father haunted her youth: her father died when she was sixteen. Dimly aware of the pain she was in, there were four months (February-June 2020) in which I slowed myself down when interacting with my daughter so that I was able to respond to her with love, validation, and assurance. This response has softened both of us—and not only that, but my daughter's physical growth has also kicked in, which has led to her body blossoming into growth. This is how we are designed: when we are struggling and in constant fear, our growth system shuts down and pushes all resources to the sympathetic nervous system so we can stay alert for survival. We are not meant to live under the condition of stress long-term. We are unable to grow our emotional intelligence if we're stuck in survival mode. This is true for all of us: the longer we feel safe, the more we're able to move towards personal growth and maturity.

Abraham Maslow, an American psychologist and philosopher, created the well-known Hierarchy of Self-Actualization. According to him (as shown in the image below), a person's most fundamental needs must be met before they can move up to the next set of growth—towards self-actualization.

Maslow's hierarchy is the foundation of the USA social services structure. Think about a homeless person, for example: they first need their physiological needs of air, water, food, shelter, and sleep to be met before they can seek safety through employment and health resources. Maslow's idea suggests that the most basic level of needs must be met before the individual will strongly desire (or focus their motivation upon) the secondary or higher-level needs.

Self-Actualization – Self Fulfillment
The desire to be their best self – to reach their potential.
Esteem – Psychological Needs
Respect, self-esteem, status, recognition, strength, and freedom.
Love and Belonging – Psychological Needs
Friendship, intimacy, family, sense of connection.
Safety – Basic Needs
Personal security, employment, resources, health, property.
Physiological – Basic Needs
Air, water, food, shelter, sleep, reproduction.
Human Needs – Abraham Maslow's hierarchy of Human Needs.

Learning about myself through my interactions with my daughter has been a wonderful process. Why had I been *reacting* to my daughter's negative behavior instead of responding to her emotional chaos with understanding? Because *my ego wanted to be observed*: I wanted my own pain to be acknowledged before I would agree to hear her pain. By human default, we are unable to hear each other until we first are heard, and often, this is how relationships come to a standoff: with each person not hearing the other. So, what do we do then? How do we listen to others first when our very nature wants ourselves to be heard first?

When we have a relationship with our Creator, He listens to us; when we sit still in meditation with God, we feel heard, loved, and forgiven. He teaches us to forgive ourselves first and foremost so that we build the capacity to hear and hold space for others. We forgive others, not because they deserve it, but because it shows compassion. Forgiveness releases the hurt feelings (which turn to hate, anger, bitterness, and resentment) that accumulate within our bodies and, when left unaddressed, develop dis-ease in our bodies, making us sick. Forgiveness frees us to stay healthy emotionally, physically, and spiritually. Through forgiveness, we become Jesus to those who don't know Him!

> *If you forgive the sins of any, they are forgiven them;*
> *If you retain the sins of any, they are retained.*
> —John 20:23

> *However, I say to you, love your enemy, bless the one who curses you, do something wonderful for the one who hates you, and pray for those who spitefully use you and persecute you,*
> *For that will reveal your identity as children of your heavenly Father;*
> *for He makes His sun rise on the evil and on the good and sends rain on the just and on the unjust.*
> —Matthew 5:44-45

> *Judge not, and you shall not be judged.*
> *Condemn not, and you shall not be condemned.*
> *Forgive (release) and you will be forgiven (released).*
> —Luke 6:37

What do you do when your own pain is too great for you to stop and listen to someone else's pain? Here's a guiding principle for these situations: the person with the highest level of awareness needs to stop and listen to the other person first.

I begin with a prayer seeking the guidance and support of the Holy Spirit. There is also a diaphragmatic breathing technique that is extremely powerful for releasing pent-up emotions in the body, and I've additionally experienced powerful healing using sound-healing (energy-moving work that uses the soundwaves in music to release energy stuck in the body). This may be why some people love to play instruments and *feel* music: music is vibrational, and we are vibrational beings. Energy is vibrational; our voices are vibrational. We send out soundwaves when we speak in the same way that music sends out soundwaves as it plays. Our bodies embrace these soundwaves and they ripple into us, creating emotion (energy-in-motion).

Recently, I realized that there were things I knew I needed to do, yet I'd been unable to do them: somehow, there was a block preventing me from creating a breakthrough in my business. I had several mentors with whom I shared all I did, and each said I was doing everything right—yet there was a huge block in me, and I couldn't understand it. Finally, that beautiful soul I mentioned earlier from a business mentoring program reached out to me. She said, "I've heard your cry, and it touched me deep within; it was a cry of being blocked. I hope you don't mind me reaching out, but everything inside me told me I needed to. Are you open to me helping you?" Of course, being the personal growth junkie I am, I said a resounding, "Yes, please!" It turned out that her specialty was an extremely effective energy-healing technique named Primordial Energy Activation and Transcendence (P.E.A.T), discovered in 1999 and supporting the idea that every physical or emotional problem is rooted in one's energy system. It maintains that any problem can be solved on a deep level by removing energetic distortions, and it employs a combination of psychology, acupressure, and energetic healing by activating your primordial energy and neutralizing the emotional charge. This work has allowed my mind to slow down, and now, I am finally able to relax. I was told for years that I had a fast brain, but I couldn't comprehend what that meant; my mind and pace of thinking was all I knew. Once my body was able to release that locked energy, however, I found myself in a new state of calm: it was like a car constantly being in overdrive and thinking that was normal. It wasn't until I experienced a release that I realized how fast my mind had kept me racing to prevent me from feeling.

All these healing modalities (transformational breath; P.E.A.T; even laughter, music, and singing) have something in common: they release pent-up, negative energy trapped in the body. These modalities all use tools that support God's universal Law of Vibration. I am certain there are other effective energy healing modalities, but the ones I've listed here are what I've personally worked with and found to be incredibly helpful.

Laughter and singing are both energy-in-motion: they send high-frequency soundwaves through our vocal cords and bodies and out into the world to embrace other people. Those high-frequency soundwaves release energy within while also sending energy into the vibrational being of others. This creates a response in others, moving energy through their bodies, too!

Similarly, laughter and smiles are simply contagious! Have you ever experienced the moment when you are in a bad mood and then someone gives you a genuine smile? If so, what happened? Your spirit began to lift! You began to feel seen, and you may have smiled back. At least one piece of you and your spirit was lifted higher. This is because we need each other; we were designed and created to need other people. We need love, laughter, understanding, and acceptance—the third tier in Maslow's Hierarchy of Human Needs: Love and Belonging. When we can set aside our anger and try to *understand* what another person is going through, it connects us, and we suddenly have compassion and understanding for them. We may even feel love and a sense of belonging as a result. It's hard to have such empathy for others on our own, but with the power of the Holy Spirit dwelling in us, we are transformed through the Spirit and the essence of love, evidenced by the production of love, joy, peace, patience, kindness, goodness, faith, modesty, and self-control in us.

Perhaps this attempt at understanding what another is going through is the motivation behind the current movement Black Lives Matter: people in the United States and around the world are beginning to pause, reflect, and realize that the disregard shown to some could be directed to each one of us just as easily. Suddenly, we are noticing the injustices black lives face, rather than sweeping them under the carpet and dismissing them without first pausing to observe and listen. There's power in listening, observing, and trying to understand another perspective. We must remember our history to prevent it from repeating and behave accordingly.

Remember this: The only thing needed for evil to reign is for a good man to do nothing! Injustice done to one person can easily be done to another. History gives us many examples of this; just think of Hitler and World War II with the attack on the Jews with Shoah (also known as the Holocaust), where an excess of six million Jews was annihilated. Always stand for love above all!

CHAPTER 6:
THE CONSCIOUS AND
SUBCONSCIOUS MIND

THINK ABOUT THIS: HUMANS ARE the only living creatures born into this world one hundred percent helpless and at the mercy of others. The majority of animals and mammals can stand and run within minutes of arriving in this world—not doing so is a matter of life or death, after all!—while humans, despite being at the top of the food chain, are completely vulnerable and dependent on others at birth. We come in this world able to breathe and with exceptional physical intelligence that keeps our physical bodies functioning for us (heart beating, blood flowing, organs working, etc.), and yet our minds are essentially empty slates at birth.

Scientists now understand that we are constantly absorbing everything in our environments from conception to about seven years of age. Think about babies: they learn to speak like the people around them, mimicking the sounds (accents) they hear and developing the mannerisms and thought patterns of those they grow up around or genetically inherit from.

To think about the conditions and beliefs under which we grew up and how our unconscious minds are programmed is intriguing. Think about our amazing physical intelligence that functions independently to keep us alive. As infants and children, we have no regulator to guide or guard what we are being told and whether our experience is good or bad; rather, our early experiences are all we know and thus become our standard/default, much like a computer that comes with preprogrammed functionality.

In a nutshell, we are born into the world virtually empty and get programmed through our caregivers, which becomes our default mode. These programs come down from generations, picked up at the unconscious level at conception through to seven years of age, and then control our lives, limiting what opportunities we see as being available to us. This is a repetitive cycle passed onto our children.

It's not until the time we reach seven years of age that our conscious minds (the gatekeeper) are developed. Up to that time, we are blank slates accepting as truth all that we experience. Fascinating and yet scary, when you think of the ramifications!

It's one thing to understand something intellectually; it's quite another to apply it to your life. While I understood this human development cycle, I did not consider what that meant to me as an individual. I did not stop to think about how this was impacting my life today. As I listened to others' stories and began to share my life experiences and stories with others, however, I gained insight into the depth of the dysfunction and pain I grew up with. It would, however, be another thirty-seven years before I uncovered the unconscious beliefs that were filtering what opportunities I saw as being available to me. Unconscious beliefs that limited my choices and beliefs were guiding my experiences in such a way where those beliefs would inevitably be validated.

You see, that's what the unconscious mind does with the beliefs (or programs) it has been given: it uses them to guide our lives to keep us on track for those beliefs to stay true! This is both a blessing and a curse: if we have Truth programmed in our subconscious, we will live a solid, productive life; but if we have lies programmed, we will be living out our lives as if those lies are true—and because they are in our subconscious minds, we don't even realize they are lies or that they are guiding and limiting our options/choices! The Bible refers to these false beliefs as false doctrines and strongholds in our minds that must be pulled down.

Allow me to share a few of my childhood experiences—things that were a part of my daily life that I thought were normal. I had nothing to tell me they were not normal; it was all I knew!

- Growing up with my siblings fighting with knives, chairs, brooms, and water hoses. We lived in a corner house and due to the angles and curves in the streets, we could see four other blocks from our front yard. Walking home from my friend's home one afternoon, I turned the corner and could hear and see my brother and sister fighting in the yard with chairs, brooms, etc. It dawned on me that day that it was a little crazy!

- I remember one summer; our family attended a family campground with some of my dad's acquaintances. I was about six years of age, and I recall that when night fell, all the men disappeared. My mom, siblings and I were sitting around a campfire when I realized that there were no men at any of the campsites; just moms and kids. My curious, adventurous self snuck away to look for my dad, uncle, and the rest of the men. When I found them, I witnessed a huge circle of men in white gowns with white hoods encircling a 12-foot burning cross. That image of a burning cross encircled by white-robed men is forever engraved in my memory. In panicky confusion, I ran around the campground into a nearby community room, where I found more men sitting in white garbs. I heard one man ask, "Whose little redhead is this?" Another man said, "That's L.N.'s baby girl." Later, I would recognize those voices, discover the nature of the group of men, and come to the horrific understanding that one of the men was the pastor in the local church that preached hell, fire, and brimstone on Sunday mornings. How could that be? How could a preacher who taught the love of God be involved in such activities? Looking back, I now realize that the preacher didn't talk of God's love at all; he talked only of Satan's hell. Talk about disturbing realizations! Feelings of insecurity and lack of trust were naturally borne from an experience like this. So how would this belief (i.e., "I cannot trust anyone") be reflected in my daily life and filter how I saw the world? How would this foundation of anger and sadness show up in my life? Later, I was told that during that weekend, when my oldest sister was at home while the rest of the family went camping, our front doorbell rang and my sister was greeted by the FBI. They began interrogating her about the location of our dad. It turned out that my dad was affiliated with the Knights of the Ku Klux Klan (KKK). This group performed horrific tragedies. Please see https://www.dictionary.com/'s definition of the Ku Klux Klan below.

Ku Klux Klan [koo-kluhks-klan] SHOW IPA

noun

1. *U.S. History.* a secret hate group in the southern U.S., active for several years after the Civil War, which aimed to suppress the newly acquired rights of Black people and to oppose carpetbaggers from the North, and which was responsible for many lawless and violent proceedings.

2. Official name **Knights of the Ku Klux Klan.** a secret hate group inspired by the former, founded in 1915 and currently active across the U.S., especially in the South, directed against Black people, Muslims, Jews, Catholics, foreign-born individuals, and other groups.

A secret society dedicated to the supremacy of white people in the United States. It began in the South during the time of Reconstruction and attempted to terrorize the many southern blacks and carpetbaggers who had replaced white southerners in positions of power. The Klan gained renewed strength in the 1920s and again in the 1960s but is now very diminished. It has stated that it aims to preserve "pure Americanism." It has attacked Jews (see also Jews) and Roman Catholics, along with immigrants and communists but is still primarily opposed to equal rights for black people and has often engaged in violence against them. Klansmen wear white hoods and robes. Klan leaders have titles such as Grand Dragon, Grand Cyclops, and Imperial Wizard.

A favored tactic of Klansmen is to burn a wooden cross outside the house of someone whom they wish to intimidate. Typically, they want the occupant to move out of the vicinity. The burning cross is a threat of future assaults if the victim does not do what the Klan wants.

- My oldest brother being a magician. To support my older brother, my mother painted our two-car garage door into a business card for my oldest brother, known as Wendell the Wizard. This seemed normal to me—only it later materialized that Mom painted the garage door out of guilt. My older sister later told me my mom was an angry woman and abusive towards her two oldest children (Wendell and Deborah), and having had counseling, she had been trying to reconcile and improve her relationship with them at that time. Painting the garage door and helping my brother solicit work, therefore (according to my oldest sister), was the result of Mom's guilt, not of the love and support of a caring mother. This I find interesting: Mom would tell stories of her childhood and how she was poorly treated and controlled by guilt, and so to hear my sister say Mom was acting out of guilt would, indeed, be true to her patterns of thinking. My oldest sister to this day also uses guilt to try to get others to conform to what she wants them to do.

As I reflect on our family dynamics, I can see the behavioral patterns repeated through the generations. This holds true to what is scientifically proven: that we pass our beliefs down through the generations through our children and great-grandchildren for up to five generations. It is indeed intriguing when I pause and reflect on my children and I see myself and my (some now old) patterns in their behaviors, too.

I try to have empathy toward others; to walk in their moccasins and understand their vantage point. I have learned to have compassion for others and to harbor the knowledge that they did the best they could at that moment in time considering their level of growth.

Perhaps my oldest brother never forgave my mother for his early childhood experiences—which would be interesting, since this would be directed at just our mother and not at both our mother and father. Perhaps this is because it's the mothers who mostly stay present in raising the children, the father's absence leading to their responsibility (or lack thereof) being overlooked.

Understanding Mother: Unwanted and Unloved
This cycle of intergenerational pain is very well-demonstrated by my mother's behavior. My mom was an educated woman. She grew up in Vincennes, Indiana, and graduated high school. She lived in New York for a while and somehow ended up in Detroit, where she met my dad.

There was another man interested in my mom, or so the story goes: Mom has told me the story many times of how my dad chased off the other man interested in her.

I'm the youngest of five. Mom was in college working on her bachelor's degree when she fell pregnant with me—which is perhaps why I have a love of education! Mom went on to get her master's degree and took courses that allowed her to travel abroad to Egypt, Israel, England, and many other countries.

Most of the moms in the neighborhood in which I grew up were full-time housewives, but my mom was a third-grade teacher. My friend Michelle's mom was a high school librarian, and I think these were the only two women in the neighborhood who worked outside of the home for many years. One mom was a hairstylist and had a beautiful salon in her basement, so even though she worked, she was still home all day and only took clients by appointment. What a time (the 1960 and 1970s) to remember!

My maternal grandmother, Alberta, lived in Vincennes, Indiana, and was extremely outspoken, opinionated, and judgmental. My mother, Ellen, felt very unloved by her mother: she would consistently share stories of how unloved and unwanted she was growing up. Even when I was fully grown, my mother (then in her sixties) would still tell us stories of how unloved she was. Sometimes, my mom said she felt more like a younger sister to my grandmother than a daughter.

Grandma lived to be in her nineties, though we only saw her about once or twice a year. When she came to our home in Michigan, her visit was always preceded by a week-long frantic cleaning of the house—and yet no matter how hard we worked to clean the house, Grandma would consistently make negative comments. That's why my mom felt she could do nothing right in the eyes of her mother. When we visited Grandma in Indiana, it was like a museum: spotless.

She got up so early that no one ever saw her clean! She was also a gourmet chef, catering for women's groups at the church.

I understand that Mom did the best she could in her life. I believe everyone is doing the best that they can with where they are at during each moment of life. We are all controlled by the unconscious beliefs we absorbed through our parents, siblings, and those we spent time with in our early childhood, so it's no real fault of our own; it is our design. That is, until we wake up to those unconscious beliefs that were passed down to us.

While my father was the youngest of fourteen, my mom was an only child and felt unwanted, unloved, and totally unsupported her entire life. According to court documents and dates, my maternal grandmother became pregnant out of wedlock, who left my mom with her (my grandmother's) parents. Hence, my mother was raised by her grandparents for many years, until one year, when she was "shipped off" to a Catholic boarding school for girls. This was a poor experience and ultimately left a bad memory for my mother. She often told the story and added, "And we weren't even Catholic!" She talked of how strict the nuns were; how they would punish the girls; how she wanted to run away.

Essentially, my mom felt judged by her mother as "never good enough". This is interesting, because these are some of the beliefs *I* have unconsciously held during my life, and I also believe my children may hold these beliefs. Recently, during twelve weeks of therapy releasing trapped negative emotion and energy in my body, I uncovered many of my unconscious beliefs. Here's a list. You may find you hold some of these, too!

- I am alone.
- I have no one to help me.
- I cannot trust anyone.

- I am rejected, unwanted, and unworthy. (This implies that I must always pay and keep paying, as no one would care enough to help me just for being a fellow human.)
- I am ashamed. (Shame is a powerful limiting belief that is only powerful when kept hidden in the dark; once the light and truth are shined upon it, it disappears like a shadow.)
- If I slow down my brain, I will become mentally disabled. (This came from observing at a young age a neighbor who had a son who was born with disabilities and a younger daughter who was born healthy. The parents treated the girl as if she were also disabled and held her back so she could engage with her brother, and in light of this, my mother explained how people can be conditioned to limit their thinking from an early age.)
- I can't...
- I have no control; I must comply.
- Something must be wrong with me.
- I cannot get "free" help from others, or they will think I am greedy. (This belief initially carried over into business: if I charge what my services are worth, others will think I'm greedy.)

Even as I review this list now, I can see that these same beliefs exist in both of my parents.

Understanding My Dad's Family: Land-Rich, Cash-Poor

My father was born in the northern Blue Ridge Mountains, a segment of the Northern Appalachian Mountain Range in Suches, Georgia. It's beautiful land, now referred to as "The Valley Above the Clouds". The area is widely known for its abundant scenic views, and as a child, Dad would take me and my siblings to Georgia during the summer (and sometimes Easter break) to visit his sister, my Aunt Gladys, while he and Uncle J.M. tended to the fields. This gave my mom quiet time alone in Michigan, where I grew up.

Aunt Gladys lived in the house in which my father grew up. This home had no running water—only what was piped in from the creek, a constant stream that flowed into a red bucket with a ladle for drinking in the kitchen sink. In the late 1950s/early 1960s, my dad and Uncle J.M. tapped into the local creek that ran through our property and hooked it into the house. I can still see a clear picture in my mind of the kitchen sink with a bright red bucket under the faucet catching the ice-cold water that streamed from the creek. You couldn't turn it off. In the bathroom, they had an antique, claw-legged bathtub, even though there was no hot water in the house: if you wanted a bath, you would have to boil water in the kitchen on the wooden stove and haul it into the bathroom to pour into the tub one pot at a time. You can imagine that it would take a while to get enough water for a bath! Aunt Gladys mostly took sponge baths. While the house was ultimately upgraded with electricity, the only heat was from the two wood-burning fireplaces: one in the living room and one in the kitchen. Aunt Gladys kept her bed in the corner of the living room so she could enjoy the heat from the fireplace.

This manner of life was normal for me growing up; it wasn't until I was a teenager that I realized my friends never experienced the limitations of living in such conditions. This gave me a unique vantage point. Take, for example, this story of visiting Aunt Julie and Uncle Archie: Aunt Julie and Uncle Archie lived on the outskirts of a nearby town. I remember visiting them on a rainy day and asking to use their bathroom, upon which request Uncle Archie said, "Go out the front door and turn right. You'll see a small building on the left. It's a two-seater!" My mouth dropped open. Surely he was joking? All the adults laughed and said, "He's not kidding!" and sent me outside (through the rain) to use their two-seater outhouse! This was their normal.

In contrast, my dad's other sister (my Aunt Mabel) and her husband owned a cattle ranch with a modern brick home and all the standard amenities: an indoor bathroom with plumbing for hot/cold running water; central air conditioning; heat; gas/electric kitchen appliances. What a contrast! It was clear to me at a young age that many fundamental things we take as essential (like running hot water) are really comfortable privileges.

I realize I am speaking from a North American perspective. I suppose many of my audience who were raised outside of the United States may have grown up with similar experiences. For the United States, though, this is certainly a comfort we take for granted.

Regardless, my childhood was my normal. My father worked nights, so we rarely saw him, and if he was home, he was sleeping. On the weekends, he was mostly out with my Uncle J.M. attending events for clubs they belonged in, hunting, fishing, or doing work for one of their sister's properties.

Dad would, on occasion, be home during the weekend, and during these times, Uncle J.M. would almost always be present. The family referred to Dad and Uncle J.M. as the Siamese Twins, joined at the hip. Notably, Dad was a Mason—and a thirty-second-degree Mason, at that.

My mom and dad were married for thirty years before they divorced when I was in the eighth grade. We saw more of my dad weekly after they divorced than when they were married: Dad suddenly wanted to spend time with us each Sunday afternoon. Even my oldest sister, Deb, who had been living on her own for years, would show up at Dad's to hang out and eat dinner with us. Wendell, my oldest brother (eleven years older than me) was already married and didn't come over; in fact, Wendell may have already been in the army and living in Colorado or Texas with his wife and their daughter at that time.

Dad would bake several chickens and broil several steaks and serve these alongside some vegetables. He cooked: he didn't buy out and bring it in. It was important to Dad to never run out of food. Being the youngest of fourteen growing up, I was told he always had to eat last, getting whatever was left; plus, I think he didn't want to disappoint us. Dad never expressed his love in words; instead, gifts (usually in the form of a twenty-dollar note or a stick of gum) were his love language.

When I was a young girl, I really liked my dad—as most girls do, I suppose, besides those in abusive or neglectful situations (though even in abusive situations there are often mixed emotions). Everyone loved my dad, and I do mean everyone: he had a great smile, was good-looking, and was generous. He would give you the shirt off his back if you asked. Dad was a hard worker, too. I remember he always had Wrigley's Spearmint Gum to freely share in his shirt pocket.

Dad was rarely alone. As I previously said, Uncle J.M. seemed to always be either over at Dad's or out with him.

I remember my dad asking me (in the presence of Uncle J.M.) on my birthday each year, "How does anyone get so goddamn ugly in [insert age] years?" As I reflected and learned over the years, Uncle J.M. was very abusive to his wife and his daughters. Dad didn't speak to me like that normally; only when Uncle J.M. was there. My oldest sister was shocked to hear dad said this to me; she thought she was the only one he said that too! Hearing she wasn't alone made her feel better. Indeed, as I've grown and spoken with my older siblings, I've discovered so much about my dad that I hadn't known when I was younger.

Uncle J.M. was four or five years older than Dad and controlled just about everything, my dad assuming the role of the compliant younger brother. My dad notably didn't get past the third grade, and so my dad's access to outside education was essentially limited, leaving just his environment to learn from—something that significantly hindered his development, I'm sure.

Our lesson from these stories? The wounds we carry with us get pushed down into our subconscious and continue to control us for a long time after they are inflicted upon us. They limit what we see in the world and the opportunities that register with us. We get what we're looking for, and our subconscious mind absorbs so many rules so well that in everything we do, we subconsciously create results that confirm the beliefs we hold.

By the time I hit junior high and high school, I was incredibly angry with my father: I didn't like his biases or the way he treated my mom or us children. He neglected us, and it seemed he was never there for us; it always seemed that my father prioritized Uncle J.M. over us, as well as his older sister, Aunt Gladys, who he would always provide with financial assistance. Dad and Uncle J.M. would complete the fourteen-hour drive to Georgia twice a year, minimum, to work the land, support Aunt Gladys, and sponsor the annual Wilkins Family Reunion each Memorial Day weekend. (As I recall it, my mother was not happy about the timing of this reunion; clearly, these things were priorities for Dad, even though the Wilkins Family Reunion always took place around, or during, my mother's birthday.)

When my oldest daughter, Tabetha, was two years old, I took her to a family reunion in Georgia. Cousins, aunts, uncles, siblings, nieces, and nephews were all staying at my dad's home. He had moved back to Georgia after him and my mother had divorced and married a woman from his youth. It was great to see the family: even my oldest brother Wendell and his wife and four kids were there. At the end of the week, everyone left except me and my daughter; we stayed a second week. Boy, what an experience! I was a single mom living in

Southern California and was dating a black man, Charles, at the time. My dad would have freaked out if he knew. Tabetha, my oldest daughter, is half Puerto Rican, and my siblings were concerned before this family visit that dad would reject her: one drop of blood that wasn't "white" was a problem, or so went the staunch rhetoric we heard growing up.

During this second week, my stepmom's son made some horrific comments about black people. I don't remember the exact words; I just remember thinking, *Why has this fourteen-year-old boy who's never known any black people come up with such terrible opinions and biases?* This young boy, clearly, thoroughly believed the comments he made. It was sickening.

I realized then that he had been raised hearing these things and thus believed them one hundred percent. He knew no different; that's all he'd been exposed to.

This event made me remember growing up with my dad in Michigan and my hearing so much of that same horrific rhetoric. I didn't agree with those beliefs at the time, nor do I now, so I would verbally debate and argue with Dad. Dad found me to be humorous: he used to get a kick out of how much I would fight against him, my stance being that all people are created equal. On one occasion of my dad's biased rantings during Sunday dinner, I unabashedly fought him. My siblings called me into the living room and said, "Candie, stop fighting Dad. You don't have to get so upset. He's egging you on. It's not worth fighting with him. Just say yes and agree with him." I replied, "Yes, it is worth fighting for. *People* are worth fighting for."

My three siblings that were present that day all encouraged me to just nod my head in agreement to the biases my dad was spouting off so that Dad would stop pressing the topic, but I could bring myself to do no such thing: I knew that if I agreed with him (even just to get him to stop speaking), it would change who I was inside. I liked who I was, and I value people of all races, so I wasn't about to do that!

Lately, I've thought deeply about my reaction: why was I so staunch and unwavering? Why were my beliefs so different from my dad's, and maybe even my siblings'? Maybe because I was the youngest and my mother had been in college while I was in her womb: she took me on trips to meet her educated friends, one trip being to Chicago to meet her friend, who was a beautiful, stylish, and educated black woman she had met while traveling abroad for college credit. This beautiful woman had earned a doctorate. She was amazing: she had a fancy loft apartment in a high-rise building, and she dressed ever-so-stylishly. Indeed, through my mother, I was exposed to higher education from conception, and my mom introduced me to people of many different ethnicities to offset the prejudiced comments and beliefs spouted by my dad. Mom taught me that all people are equal and that we shouldn't judge them based on their skin or ethnicity.

I remember the Detroit riots in 1967 and 1968. Though I was only four/five years old at the time, I recall Mom putting us in the family station wagon and driving us to Detroit (we lived in the suburbs, twenty miles northeast of Detroit) to see what was happening. She told us that we shouldn't believe everything we hear in the news; that someone owns the press and it's their vantage point we are informed of. She said that the riots were creating history and that we needed to see it for ourselves. History books teach what authorities *want* you to believe, and Mom knew this—so she took us into Detroit to see things unfold firsthand. Here's a clip from a Wikipedia article on these events:

The 1967 Detroit Riot, also known as the 12th Street Riot, was the bloodiest incident in the 'long, hot summer of 1967'. Composed mainly of confrontations between black residents and the Detroit Police Department, it began in the early morning hours of Sunday July 23, 1967, in Detroit, Michigan. The 1967 Detroit Riots were among the most violent and destructive riots in U.S. history. By the time the bloodshed, burning and looting ended after five days, 43 people were dead, 342 injured, nearly 1,400 buildings had been burned and some 7,000 National Guard and U.S. Army troops had been called into service.

The scale of the riot was the worst in the United States since the 1863 New York City draft riots during the American Civil War, and was not surpassed until the 1992 Los Angeles riots 25 years later.

The 1968 Detroit riot was a civil disturbance that occurred between April 4–5, 1968 in Detroit, Michigan following the assassination of Martin Luther King, Jr. Less than a year after the violent unrest of 1967, areas of 12th Street (present-day Rosa Parks Boulevard) again erupted in chaos (simultaneously with 110 other US cities) following King's assassination. Michigan Governor George W. Romney ordered the National Guard into Detroit. One person was killed, and gangs tossed objects at cars and smashed storefront windows with three dozen fires being set. (Source: https://en.wikipedia.org/wiki/1968_Detroit_riot)

You may be wondering why my mom didn't go to Georgia for the Wilkins Family Reunions. She did in the early years: early in their marriage, she attended the trips to Georgia to support my dad, but shortly after I was born (when she was in college), she stopped going. This meant her birthday was usually spent alone in Michigan, as Dad would take us kids to Georgia for the Family Reunion. I think this confirmed my mother's belief that she was unloved. She didn't like going to Georgia because the home in which my dad grew up was where we would stay (the place with no running hot water and only the fireplace for heat).

Ultimately, Uncle J.M.'s influence (or control) over my dad's behavior was too much, and it played a big part in undermining my parents' marriage. Dad worked the night shift at Uniroyal Tires, which meant he slept during the day while we were at school, and when we got home, he was gone. During the weekends, he went out with Uncle J.M. fishing, hunting, and attending Masonic Lodge meetings (or the meetings of other groups of which he was a member). When we went camping as a family, Dad was not present: just Mom, me, and my siblings who still lived at home. Dad wasn't around for my sports events or father-daughter banquets.

I was angry at his lack of attention and his strong biases, and I refused to call him Dad; instead, I referred to him as "Father". As a teenager, I would say, "He may be my biological father, but he isn't my dad."

Years later, I found myself repeating this phrase to my ex-husband with regards to his children. This phrase was me holding a grudge for all the times Dad wasn't around. I very much thought in black-and-white at that time.

Now, looking back, I realize I do also have fond memories with my dad. No one is perfect; we are all perfectly imperfect human beings. We do the best we can with the unconscious beliefs we hold that control us. It is important to remember that our brains are designed to reconcile our behaviors and create experiences to support our unconscious beliefs. Hence, our responsibility is to question all our assumptions and reveal our unconscious beliefs. Only then can we become aware and identify those beliefs which no longer serve us, and we can find Truth—and *then* choose our path accordingly. This is a lifelong journey.

Let's stop and think about how my dad grew up and what unconscious beliefs he probably picked up: being the youngest of fourteen, he was mostly raised by his older siblings rather than by his parents, so having a lot of parental interaction was foreign to him—as it was to my mother. It's interesting that they shared that in common. As a result of his upbringing, my father clung to what he knew: his older brother, Uncle J.M., and the doctrines they were fed through the various organizations of which they and their ancestors were members. There are many ramifications and generational consequences, from sins and curses, that come from subscribing to such organizations—but that is an entirely separate topic for another book.

Do you see a pattern in my mom and dad's behavior? They both defaulted to patterns they picked up on as children.

Starting Over

The years passed. My parents separated when I was in the eighth grade and officially divorced about five years later (after thirty-five years of marriage). Dad moved back to his childhood town in Georgia and married a widow he knew from his youth, while me, my mom, and my siblings remained in Michigan. My oldest brother was in the army, stationed in Killeen, TX.

I turned eighteen in 1981. Michigan had hit a recession the prior year. During this time, I came to know someone who had moved to California and recently returned to Michigan. This person described Southern California as warm and sunny and filled with beaches, desert, and mountains, all within an hour's drive. It was described as a paradise!

Well, that was all it took: I didn't do all the research on California that I had previously done on another state I'd considered moving to, but I had firsthand word-of-mouth about the beauty of it—so just after my nineteenth birthday, I packed my two-door Chevy Chevrolet and visited the AAA office to get paper maps for my journey to California. I headed west with just my clothes, eight-track tapes, and stereo. My mom was worried, but there wasn't anything she could do: I was nineteen and ready to embrace the world. Even now, once I get an idea in my head, that's it: I laser-focus on it and make it happen.

Mom made me promise to stop each night by 6PM, check into a hotel, and call her so she knew I was safe. At that time, there had been a rash of freeway murders, which caused her a lot of fear at the prospect of her beautiful redheaded daughter driving alone over two thousand miles across the United States, not knowing anyone in California. As I reflect, my mom had been without a support system for most of her life growing up, so she knew all too well what I could run into. Now, as a mom myself, I understand her concerns and fears: I've always told my kids that life is hard, and even harder when you don't have a support structure around you.

If you ever move, be sure to get grounded in a church where you will meet people interested in growth and establish a network of friends who can live life with you!

I've now been in California for far longer than I lived in Michigan. Considering I moved from Michigan when I was so young, I don't have a lot of day-to-day communication with my siblings. I didn't travel back home to Michigan to visit family very often over the years due to financial constraints; for me, it was normal to go up to ten years between seeing my mother, siblings, or father. Hence, I was always a little surprised whenever I heard of families that would fly across countries to holidays or a wedding at the drop of a hat! To me, that was a privilege that had escaped me—and this, too, I believe was created through subconscious beliefs that limited what choices I saw as being available to me.

When I grew up, the focus for adulthood seemed to be independence rather than interdependence. When Mom travelled, she took a shuttle to the airport; she never asked anyone to drive her. Rarely did I see my mom receive help from others; only ever in the form of paid services.

When I think about my father, he was codependent on his brother (Uncle J.M.): my father was always helping his brother, sisters, and any family member. Dad rarely said no to anyone—well, except Mom. It seems Dad prioritized his brother and his childhood family over the needs of our family—his "adult family".

I developed beliefs from both my mom and my dad; after all, we all absorb beliefs from those we were surrounded with as a child. Beliefs can be different from the intellectual understandings we hold. Don't neglect to note that!

Notably, some of the unconscious beliefs I absorbed were contradictory, which causes polarization (the division of two sharply contrasting groups or sets of opinions or beliefs). Remember, actions are based on the beliefs we hold.

It was during the early 2000s, when I was in my late thirties, that I came to the realization during a group coaching session at a week-long leadership summit that I was still displaying reactive behavior borne from my relationship with my father. Initially, I was skeptical of this idea: how could my behavior still be being controlled forty years later by things I no longer thought about? Of course, this latter statement wasn't strictly true: I was still angry toward my dad for his prejudiced beliefs, insults growing up, and absence from important childhood events.

As I look back, I remember my mother asking me while I was in my twenties, "Why do you date so many different ethnic men and not white men? Are you trying to get back at your dad?" I was astounded at this: this hadn't been a conscious decision at all, and my mother's reasoning made me come across as very vindictive. In response, I explained that I was in California with no support group around me, and so I often went on dates just to have a meal! This meant I dated a wide variety of people—their ethnicities didn't matter! There hadn't been much diversity in my hometown in Michigan: we had a strong

Greek community, but I only had one girlfriend with Hispanic heritage. I grew up in a predominately white area. With this in mind, I was taken aback by my mom's question. It had honestly never crossed my conscious mind that dating men of other ethnicities may have been a roundabout way of getting back at my dad; to prove his biases and prejudice wrong. Unconsciously, however, it makes perfect sense: I hold such strong beliefs that all people are precious and deserving of respect that my behaviors are constantly seeking opportunities to confirm this truth.

People are human, made in God's image, regardless of their skin, hair, and eye color—and this is the United States, the great melting pot! Almost everyone has ancestry from another place in the world! If you trace your genes, you may be surprised to find the origins of your ancestors—so let's focus on our common ground, not on our perceived differences.

My Relationship with My Parents

I've always longed for family connection—a connection that would value celebrating each other's companionship. This, however, has always seemed out of my reach, probably due to my subconscious belief passed down from my mother that independence is always better than interdependence—a belief that likely developed in her as a result of her treatment as a young child, raised by her grandparents and then shipped off to a Catholic boarding school as a young girl due to, in her eyes, no one wanting her around. The belief she held was that she was unlovable, and I "caught" those underlying beliefs as a child without realizing it. I am grateful I have been able to see the truth and reframe my perspective: I now accept that I am loved and that people enjoy my companionship and want to spend time with me.

What are the unconscious beliefs you hold about your worth and lovability?

Indeed, I've found that many Christian parents and their married children can have difficulty when it comes to striking a balance between the concept of "leave and cleave" and honoring parents. My father seemed to have this issue—not when it came to dealing with his parents, but when it came to dealing with his siblings, to whom he was very dedicated. The Bible addresses this concept; however, today, divorce is so prevalent that it seems that the only "permanent" relationships are those formed in childhood. Partners seem to come and go nowadays.

You may have just noticed that my above statement is symptomatic of a subconscious belief. Rather, people do what people see, and what you see depends on your circle of influence. There is, indeed, a large portion of our society that still has long marriages; divorce is still the minority! Hence, it is important that you seek people who value the same things as you.

Here are some Biblical references on the topic of the parent-child and husband-wife relationship balance.

Therefore, a man shall leave his father and mother and be joined (cleave) to his wife, and they shall become one flesh.
—Genesis 2:24

Children, obey your parents in the Lord, for this is right.
—Ephesians 6:1

Honor your father and your mother, so that you may live long in the land the Lord your God is giving you.
—Exodus 20:12

There are three aspects to these Biblical references: first, the parent-child relationship is temporary, while the marriage relationship is permanent. A problem arises when these two roles are reversed: if the parent-child relationship is overpowering, the marriage is threatened. Second, the "cleave" aspect states that a man should actively pursue his wife, even after the marriage vows are spoken. There should be no closer relationship than the husband-wife relationship: not with any former friend, nor with any parent. Third, the husband and wife will become one flesh; it takes both the husband and the wife to create a single entity.

In 1979, when I was sixteen, my relationship with my parents was fractured even further. I was fortunate enough to partake in a three-week tour of England with a day trip to France as a member of The Warren Youth Chorale. It was the summer between the tenth and eleventh grades, and that same summer, my mom took a train trip to Canada and my brother, Lowell, journeyed to China.

Whenever my mum returned from one of her multiple trips abroad, she excitedly shared her photographs and stories with me and my siblings, and her trip to Canada was no different. Similarly, Lowell also excitedly shared all about China upon his return with everyone attentively listening.

When it was my turn to share my exploits, however, it felt as though no one was interested in hearing about my adventures and discoveries; after all, England was old news (Mom had previously been there), and I had only gone with The Warren Youth Chorale to sing. Hence, when I returned home and no one in my family asked me about my trip, I felt invisible. It was painful for me to not be able to share my experience. I was bitter and felt ignored and insignificant. I believe these feelings arose as a result of a small event that had occurred during my trip: a little over two weeks into the trip, student choir members were encouraged to call home to their families to give them an update about their trip and to remind them that we'd be flying home in a few days. I remember sharing with the older students and chaperones that I wasn't going to call home as no one would want to hear from me; after all, their way of saying goodbye had been to let me ride four hours to the airport with the neighbors, who we barely spoke to. However, the chaperones and older students insisted that I needed to call home, assuring my family would be happy to hear from me and that they'd be disappointed if I didn't call. Hence, I took their advice and phoned home: I dialed the operator and placed a collect call (the only way to do it in 1979). I heard the phone ring, and my mother quickly answered. The operator asked my mother if she would accept the call charges. She said yes, and without hesitation or a *Hello, how are you?* she immediately exclaimed in an irritated voice, "What's wrong? Why are you calling long-distance overseas? Do you know how expensive overseas calls are? Is something wrong?" I totally shrank and wanted to hang up right then: I felt small, unloved, and not worth the few dollars the call would cost.

Upon arrival in the airport after my flight home, I looked around for my family. I noticed the other students were greeted with smiles, hugs, and kisses while I stood there alone, seeking the faces of my loved ones. Suddenly, the same neighbor I had carpooled with on the flight out walked over and told me, in a dull voice, that his dad said I was riding home with them.

My spirits sank. It was practical—they lived right across the street—but I had the sense my family didn't care enough to make the drive into Canada to greet me after leaving home for the first time. The lack of luster in his voice added to my feeling of unwantedness.

To add insult to injury, the ride home was not a pleasant experience: it certainly reinforced my feelings of insignificance! The father lectured his son in a very loud voice the entire four-hour drive home because he slept in and missed the day trip to France—which was an additional cost paid for, yet wasted. All the while, all I could think was to wonder why my mom or siblings hadn't come to pick me up. I truly felt like I wasn't worth being picked up by my family from the airport. On reflection, it seems that this was always how my mother felt: always arranging a shuttle rather than daring to ask someone in the family to drive her to or from the airport.

This singular event left me thinking that because my family didn't care for me, I didn't need them, either. It was probably this event (and my subsequent change in mindset towards my family) that influenced my decision to move across the United States alone at age nineteen. This negative and limiting belief—that my family didn't want me and so I didn't need them—would remain buried in my unconscious and create circumstances for years that would reinforce it.

The truth is, we are not islands: we were created for connection; we need other people. We need to learn to express our disappointments and pain so we can clarify our needs and love for each other, rather than shutting down, creating stories of unwantedness, and feeling undeserving. Our birthright, created by God in His image, makes us unbelievably valuable and wanted. We don't have to do anything to deserve God's love; he cares for us and is waiting for you to acknowledge Him and invite Him into your heart, where he can comfort and heal your wounds. God starts transforming us from the inside.

Then, by constantly using your faith, the life of Christ will be released deep inside you, and the resting place of his love will become the very source and root of your life. Then you will be empowered to discover what every holy one experiences—the great magnitude of the astonishing love of Christ in all its dimensions. How deeply intimate and far-reaching is his love! How enduring and inclusive it is! Endless love beyond measurement that transcends our understanding—this extravagant love pours into you until you are filled to

overflowing with the fullness of God!
—Ephesians 3:17-19, TPT

It was while I was in my twenties that I realized that I had a choice regarding how I wanted to remember my childhood. I was at an international student social gathering, and people were sharing their childhood stories. I would listen and think, *I had that experience, too—* and this was the case for both good and bad experiences. I realized then that while I may have had many horrible experiences growing up, there were just as many, if not more, fond memories.

I thought about the images that came to mind when each person shared their life stories, and I finally realized that I could either hold onto the bad memories and let them shape who I would become, or I could hold onto the good memories and become a better person as a result. I decided then that I would choose what to focus on: the good, not the bad. I realized that whatever I focused on I would attract more of, and so by thinking about good things, God's Law of Vibration would attract other good things to me. People want to be around positive people; people want to hear fun, loving stories, not just painful stories of woe-is-me.

Finally, brethren, whatsoever things are true, whatsoever things are honest, whatsoever things are just, whatsoever things are pure, whatsoever things are lovely, whatsoever things are of good report; if there be any virtue, and if there be any praise, think on these things.
—Philippians 4:8

What did your childhood look like? Do you hold onto your fond memories? It's important that you do. I challenge you to take some time today to reflect on your childhood and early adult years and find the good, even if it's just a small moment of joy. Find it, clasp onto it, and cherish it.

Why is it important to think about good things? Being spiritual, energetic beings, we can be likened to a radio antenna, sending out sound waves and receiving frequencies from other sources. We are receptive and can determine which radio (sound) waves (frequencies) we will receive into our lives.

Think of a radio station. There are two stations: 105 FM and 106 FM. In your current area, you get to pick the radio station to which you want to listen from the stations that get reception. When you tune your radio into the available stations, you hear music that only those individuals tuned into that station can hear. Are you following me? What you listen to and absorb directly impacts your thoughts, feelings, and behavior.

So, as we train our minds to stay focused on positive things—all things pure and beautiful—we open our minds and spirits to tuning into higher frequencies of potential and love. As we stay tuned into these frequencies, we see opportunities that would otherwise be hidden from us. We only see what we are tuned into, so if we're tuned into the frequency of God's love (the highest frequency), we will have peace beyond understanding. The human state of fear cannot exist simultaneously with love and faith!

There is no fear in love, but perfect love casts out fear. For fear has to do with punishment, and whoever fears has not been perfected in love.
—1 John 4:18

Have you ever noticed the pattern whereby people who have bad experiences seem to constantly have one bad experience after another? And have you ever noticed that some people seem to have an easier life, full of positive experiences? Have you noticed that when you purchased a blue car, there were lots of blue cars like yours on the road? You had never noticed so many blue cars when you drove a white car: when you drove a white car, you instead noticed lots of white cars on the road. This demonstrates the fact that we tune into what we are focused on: where our attention goes, our energy flows. Remember, our emotions are energy! Our thoughts control our emotions, and our emotions control our behaviors. This is summed up beautifully by the following famous proverb:

> *Be careful of your thoughts,*
> *For your thoughts become your words.*
> *Be careful of your words,*
> *For your words become your actions.*
> *Be careful of your actions,*
> *For your actions become your habits.*
> *Be careful of your habits,*
> *For your habits become your character.*
> *Be careful of your character,*
> *For your character becomes your destiny.*

As can be seen here, foundational beliefs program our subconscious minds and are generationally passed down through the ages. The exception to this rule seems to be those who have been trained to think on positive things, perhaps due to their growing up in a family already focused on positive thinking, meaning they inherited such an idea into the foundational programs that sit in their subconscious and filter their perspective on life. These families are what I call the "Hallmark Families": they are supportive of one another and they raise children who seem to move further in this positive direction. Often, their children become strong leaders in society, which makes sense, since they don't have as many negative thinking patterns to overcome. On the other hand, the families that have had challenges generation after generation often continue to spiral downward.

I want to change the generational pattern for my family, and I want you to change it for your family, if needed, too. When I moved to

California at nineteen, I did so in the hopes of becoming my best self and changing the trajectory of my life and, in turn, those of my future children, grandchildren, etc.—yet when I arrived here, the unconscious belief system I had inherited came with me and continued to attempt to define my life. Regardless, I, being the rebel I am, wanted a better quality of life; I wanted to live differently to how I grew up.

Good habits are created before we even realize it: remember, our thoughts determine our words, and our words determine our actions. Our actions then create habits, and our habits create our character— and our character determines our destiny. People do what people see, so ask yourself what the people around you are seeing through your behavior. Be a positive example and lead others. More than anything, be gentle with yourself: we are perfectly imperfect humans and we simply give each day our best, embracing each moment as it comes. The goal is to constantly grow stronger in your Divine Spirit—the essence of love. So, in line with this: what are you currently tolerating in your life that puts you out of alignment with love? Take inventory and then consciously act to bring alignment in all areas of your life. Don't compartmentalize your life; integrate all areas of it to increase your confidence and authenticity. After all, we are not meant to live a compartmentalized existence: we are meant to be whole; genuine; authentic; to live our lives out loud in all areas—and this can be done!

Notably, we may have different areas of our lives that are in alignment with our values, and some that are not. It takes intentional action to live a congruent life and to set strong boundaries that others respect. How often do you pause and tune into how your physical body is feeling? Most don't, whereas those who frequently practice yoga and/or transformational breathwork do. The average person is rushing through their day or numbing themselves on social media, movies, gaming, or substances.

When we pause to listen to our bodies, they can tell us a lot about the emotions we're feeling—which can ultimately give us clues into the unconscious thoughts and assumptions we may be living by. I wonder how much pain you're currently tolerating in your life without you even knowing it.

As with all other chapters thus far, and in light of the above, please take this moment to refer to your companion guide and complete the exercises. It is so important that you tune into yourself frequently and take a moment to acknowledge, absorb, and make peace with all of your incoming thoughts and feelings.

CHAPTER 7:
OUR RESPONSIBILITY:
RESPONSE TO ABUSE

T HE STORY I HAVE GONE into above brings us nicely to our next
topic of discussion.

You see, my history with this neighbor family—the one that
drove me home from my trip with The Warren Youth Chorale—is
another story in and of itself. The mother, Frieda, was my babysitter
before kindergarten. I adored her and her youngest son, J. This family
had five boys who all happened to closely line up with the ages of me
and my four siblings—meaning each child in our family went to school
with one of their boys.

My siblings are all between four and eleven years older than me,
and considering they were all in school during the mornings and Mom

was at work, I would be babysat at Frieda's home. Being there with my best friend J was great—until he started kindergarten. The year he turned five (1967), life there changed: Frieda's second son JK, who was a teenager, was a bully, and he did very inappropriate sexual things to me when I was only four years old, alone in the house. JK, who was around nine years older than me, would get home from school before anyone else and would convince his mom to go outside to water the front yard, stating he would watch me, before forcing me to go in the bathroom and do things with him. He was also a very effective manipulator: one of his favorite things to do was to walk me to the hallway near the living room so I could see his mom outside watering the lawn and say, "You want to call her? Go ahead; she won't hear you. She's not coming in to save you. You're mine, and you'll do whatever I tell you. Do you understand?"

Think about the imprint that left on my young, unconscious mind! Why do I share this? Because there are men and women in this world who have been abused and victimized, so while you will always hear me say you must be one hundred percent responsible for your life and your choices, the fact still stands that there are predators and there is victimization. Considering it is most certainly *not* my aim to make you feel like you're to blame for the times in which you were made a victim when I say you are one hundred percent responsible for what happens to you, I share this story to make it clear that I understand that *you cannot control the abuse that happened to you as a youth.* Be gentle with yourself. While you did not have a choice as a child with what happened, as an adult, you now do have a choice regarding how you embrace and process the ramifications of such events. When making this choice, it's important to embrace your inner child and comfort him/her; to let the inner child know you are sorry for what happened to him/her and that you, as an adult, are ready to listen to him/her and comfort their pain. Our spirits do not have the concept of time that this physical world does. The inner child, therefore, is still wounded within us. We have the responsibility to heal.

At the end of the day, inappropriate actions were directed towards me when I was only four years old, and there was nothing I could do about it at the time. I felt trapped and at his beck and call, and I dreaded the afternoons when he would arrive home before anyone else. I recall seeing my siblings arrive home from school in the early afternoon, and I would stand at the backyard fence calling to them from across the street, begging and crying for them to pick me up and bring me home. They would respond by telling me I had to stay there until Mom got home from work. They didn't want to babysit me, and I don't blame them for that; they were young and wanted their afternoon free without babysitting their little sister. I am sure they didn't know what I was being put through.

Regardless, I truly dreaded those afternoons, and the emotional pain of these events would continue to impact my life until I chose to embrace and release them. When I was in my forties, I fell in love with my then-boss, and he said he loved me, but he was not available. This weighed on me heavily, and I ultimately had to draw a line in the sand and tell him not to engage in personal discussions with me, since he was not available. I was not going to be "held captive" to a man who would never be mine. This was an emotionally triggering time, and I couldn't figure out why I was so deeply and spiritually wounded. After two years of keeping my distance, hearing him speak outside my office door to other team members about his personal life led to me slumping on the floor of my office sobbing in a fetal position: I was experiencing flashbacks of JK and the things he had done to me at four. I felt trapped, wounded, and as if I had no control to change the circumstances. In the end, I dragged myself up to my desk chair and immediately sought out a counselor through my insurance, as I knew I needed help with dealing with the intensity of my pain. I was surprised at all the things that came to my awareness; things I had repressed!

Repression, in psychoanalytic theory, [is] the exclusion of distressing memories, thoughts, or feelings from the conscious mind. Often involving sexual or aggressive urges or painful childhood memories, these unwanted mental contents are pushed into the unconscious mind.
—https://www.britannica.com/science/repression-psychology

I recalled a time when I was eight years old riding my bike in my neighborhood. JK walked by and pushed me off my bicycle, and I landed in a muddy puddle while he called me filthy names. I was humiliated and had to walk a block home, past several other children my age playing and laughing in their yards, who saw me cry, covered in mud. I felt small, insignificant, and unloved. I felt unsafe. I was afraid the other children were laughing at me as I walked by, as if I deserved it. JK's behavior was cruel and mean, and this I repressed as well—but now, it was bubbling to the surface so that I could take one hundred percent responsibility for my feelings and deal with the false beliefs my unconscious mind had created, and replace them with God's Truth of who I am and how worthy of love I am.

To help you to do this, you can use the following as a reminder. Feel free to copy this down and carry it with you as a physical token of your identity in Christ.

Because of Christ's redemption,
I am a new creation of infinite worth.
I am deeply loved,
I am completely forgiven,
I am fully pleasing,

I am totally accepted by God.
I am absolute complete in Christ.
When my performance
reflects my new identity in Christ,
that reflection is dynamically unique.
There has never been another person like me
in the history of mankind,
nor will there ever be.
God has made me an original,
one of a kind, really somebody!

As I look back through my life at the injustices done to me, God has consistently intervened and held those who've hurt me responsible without me having to do anything: in this situation, JK passed away in his twenties after falling out of a tree he was trimming. He'd had a steady girlfriend and a child, and when I heard of his death, I felt that this may have been God's way of handling vengeance and preventing any further damage to others.

Many of you have similar stories, and far worse. Perhaps you can understand and/or relate to my pain and humiliation. You may feel a stirring within you and even recollect something that you have suppressed. You may feel deep emotion and not know why you are experiencing this. Reading my experience may trigger memories of your own. It's time for you to stop suppressing those memories and to acknowledge them to release your inner pain.

Emotional suppression is a type of emotional regulation strategy that is used to try and make uncomfortable, overwhelming thoughts and feelings more manageable. There are many different emotion regulation strategies, and some are more helpful than others.

Many people with borderline personality disorder (BPD) will report that they spend a lot of time and energy suppressing emotions. If you have ever had an intense thought or feeling that you couldn't handle in the moment and tried

to push it away, you have experienced emotional suppression. Research shows that not only is it ineffective in eliminating thoughts and feelings, but it may even worsen the situation.
—https://www.verywellmind.com/suppressing-emotions-425391

You have a choice; it's *your* responsibility how you handle your emotions. When bad things happen, we naturally hold our breath, which traps the feelings and the stimuli around us in that moment into the cells of our body—and when they are trapped within us, they continue to haunt us and cause emotional and physical pain. We can, however, confront the pain, release the trapped emotions, and receive peace and healing—or we can choose to hold onto the pain and continue to repress those memories, which will result in health issues down the road—if they haven't already.

Only you can choose how to handle your emotions: you can choose to suppress and repress, or you can choose to embrace the feelings and receive healing. No one can heal your pain for you; you have the choice to heal, and that requires your full participation. When Jesus healed people in the Bible, He asked them if they *wanted* to be healed; He involved them in the process. They had to choose health; they had to express their faith.

You may need someone with you to hold space for you and guide you through this process, as it is a powerful experience. This may be scary, so be brave and find someone to help you. Freedom is on the other side of pain, and resetting your mind and body is so worth the journey.

I'll always remember the day I left my counselor's office in 2004 and suddenly experienced an onslaught of severe flashbacks of being four years old and experiencing the things JK exposed me to. The pain was real. I was reliving those experiences thirty-eight years later as if they were happening then. I was paralyzed with fear, just as scared at forty-two years of age as I had been at four and eight. Even though JK was dead and I knew that at the back of my mind, emotionally, I was trapped in the feelings of my younger self; my inner wounded child. It wouldn't be until fifteen years later that I would truly release the negative emotion trapped in my body associated with these events. The key here is to sit with these feelings and let them flow—just the feelings. Don't go back into seeing the events; just feel the sadness and fear.

This can be difficult, which is why I recommend getting a professional to assist you in the process. You can begin by scanning your body to tap into your bodily sensations, and when you find a sensation (e.g., pain; pressure; tightness), stop and ask yourself what the emotion that is tied to the bodily sensation is. You may be surprised at what turns up. You may have a flashback, but if that happens, immediately focus on the arising emotion and let go of the event's details; merely focus on the sadness, fear, rejection, etc. that arises, as these feelings will resolve after several minutes and be replaced with peace. Don't buy into the story; don't replay the events: just sit with the pain and fear and let it move out of the cells of your body. You may even experience a physical shaking as the energy releases, which is a good sign.

Our emotions do not know time; they are simply energy-in-motion which, when repressed or suppressed, get stored in our bodies, pushed down, and blocked from our conscious minds. This energy doesn't go away: it stays frozen in time with all the memories and sensations that were tied to it when it happened. The memories reside in our subconscious and continue to control us, and anything in our daily lives that resembles one of the senses that was captured and stored in our cells at the time of the distressing event will automatically trigger our unconscious into a feeling of insecurity.

Emotions are a tool to help us to understand where we are in connection to the present—our current circumstances—and our real connection with God. Many of us are stuck in the past, controlled by unconscious emotions that we don't even realize. There is so much more to life when we live in awareness and practice being in the moment. When we are not in a state of joy, we can use our emotions as a guide to help us get back on track. Our original design is to live in a state of joy and peace, which is possible when we are consciously connected to God.

When you experience one of the sensory sensations that trigger those emotions that were felt at the time of the event in question, decide whether it is a good memory that you want to enjoy by reminiscing or reliving the experience. If, alternatively, the memory is bad, you still have a *choice* in terms of how you respond. You can continue to be angry, scared, bitter, and to suppress it one more time, or you can choose to ask God to help you to resolve that matter once and for all. Remember, it's one hundred percent your choice how you respond.

The ability to repress and suppress things into our unconscious mind is a protective gift God designed in us; it's a protective measure to capture these sensations so that your brain can protect you and keep you in a survival state, should you come across that same situation later. Then, when things are calmer, your memory will bring the sensations back to you so you can resolve the matter.

Take the initiative and reframe the matter. Reflect and figure out what is good and what is bad. This is an opportunity to develop insight and wisdom that you can carry with you through this life to be a better, stronger person. God never wants you to be bitter; to carry hurt; to be angry from resentment. God didn't design our memories to hurt us! The negative events we experience are part of the human plight and the fallen state of the world.

The Lord is my protector; he is my strong fortress. My God is my protection, and with him I am safe. He protects me like a shield; he defends me and keeps me safe.
—Psalm 18:2

It is my goal to share my personal stories with you while simultaneously educating you on how our brain and parasympathetic nervous system work. Together, stories and education can be memorable tools and can be put to great use. Let's not let shame keep our stories hidden. Shame occurs and grows when we keep our stories in the dark.

Shame typically comes up when you look inward with a critical eye and evaluate yourself harshly, often for things you have little control over. This negative self-evaluation often has its roots in messages you've received from others, especially during your childhood.
—https://www.healthline.com/health/mental-health/toxic-shame

Shame disappears when it is exposed to the light. Sharing our stories is healing, both for us and for those who hear our stories. Not everyone wants to read a scientific book on how the brain works, and many also don't want to read stories of abuse alone—and yet when we combine our stories with the facts of how our bodies work—how God designed us—we create a unique bridge that some will embrace.

God has designed us beautifully. We are imperfectly perfect and perfectly imperfect! The way God created us is truly an amazing thing.

We think we are broken when we have sudden, strong emotions hit us, when in actuality, those emotions are God saying, "My daughter/son, let's go back and heal something." Embrace the emotion and ride it like a rollercoaster! It may be difficult, but it's a necessary process. It's okay to find time when you are alone to sit in the pain; to cry, to holler—whatever you must do to grieve and release the trapped emotion. In other countries, wailing walls are employed—which feature in the Bible, too—since people *have to grieve.*

We need to realize that our emotions are beautiful and that it is okay to feel. Feelings are natural; neutral; normal; and they do not define us. Our feelings are a gift to let us know if we are on the right track to staying connected to joy; to God; just like the GPS in your vehicle tells you if you are following its directions properly or if you are off-course. The GPS system can't drive the car for you; you must make the choice of whether to follow the guidance or not—and in the same way, you have the choice of whether or not to follow the guidance of your emotional GPS system, or to keep going in your own direction by suppressing emotions. Even though the GPS relentlessly offers new choices at every corner, it cannot make the decisions for you; you, as a human, have free will and the responsibility to choose. If you choose not to decide, you are still deciding.

I know it's hard to know the right decision at times, but remember, if you are tuned into God as your Creator, He will walk with you and make sure to turn everything that happens to you into a good thing, somehow—even the bad things! If you stay close to God, He will provide you with the means and measures to survive and to even go beyond survival. God wants you to thrive; to enjoy the abundance of this life; to see the beauty in this world; to develop beautiful relationships; to have positive experiences.

> *Trust in the Lord with all your heart,*
> *And lean not on your own understanding;*
> *In all your ways acknowledge Him,*
> *And He will make your paths straight.*
> —Proverbs 3:5-6

Remember the six faculties—memory, reason, perception, imagination, intuition, and will—give you all the resources you need to dream and design your life. Are you willing to explore these faculties?

Design, in your mind, the life you want to live. Consider drawing or painting pictures of that life, either in your imagination or on paper, using images or words through journaling. As you create those images of the life of your dreams, you are creating images—memories—of your future. As you create those images, imagine the feelings that go along with living your ideal life. Experience joy, peace, happiness, and love.

God created within you a psycho-mechanism that takes those preconceived memories and pushes them into your subconscious (just like the terrible experiences you had that got stored into your subconscious and began ruling your life with fear when triggered by smells or sounds reminding you of the past bad events).

Remember, our minds and memories do not track time, so if the memory is one from the past or a memory of something you created in your imagination, the subconscious mind will not be able to tell the difference. Do you realize the power of this knowledge? You can create memories of your future life and build powerful "truths" in the subconscious of your mind so that your mind will create opportunities to reinforce the truth of these future memories!

Indeed, God wants you to use the six faculties He gifted you with to create the life of your dreams. You can do this! You can create smells, sounds, colors, images, tastes, and even the sense of feeling textures; you can build memories of a future life that you want to live. Build it first in your imagination. As you do this, the subconscious will grab hold of this imagery and begin to work on it for you, slowly showing you opportunities that will make this "memory" come true in your physical world. Remember, the programs in your subconscious run your life; they are doing ninety-five percent of your brain's functioning for you each day. This is such a gift! There is so much going on in this world that it would be overwhelming if you had to consciously do everything through your own will each day.

God is with you to guide and support you. Develop the gift of your six faculties. Now is the time: with the COVID pandemic, the world literally shut down for months and people were inadvertently gifted with the opportunity to take a break and reassess their lives. Many took this time to reflect, learn, and dream of something better.

Now is a time of reflection worldwide. Mankind is out of control, with families running ragged with their schedules and new technology taking over our lives as we grow more dependent on them. It's important to assess what you are doing and what habits you've created and to acknowledge why you are doing them. Often, we do things just because we can: we can automate and/or have more of an income by both parents working, so we do it without thinking about the consequences of our choices. We also do things due to the expectations others put on us.

Ask yourself: Is that necessary? Is it good?

Who is raising your children? Why did you have children? Do you want to have a bigger impact on the lives of your children than you currently do? What happens when your children are taken from you at a young age? What happens when the court system intrudes into your life and takes over, limiting your time and the way in which you interact with your children? What happens when you see your children hurting and you know you have the love they need but are not allowed to access them? What happens when you see life passing by and you can't get it back? What happens then?

My mid-forties to -fifties were a difficult time in my life: I wanted nothing more than to be a mom, love my children, and raise them to know God. I am blessed and fortunate enough to be able to say that God made it possible for my two youngest children to attend a private Christian elementary school so that they could be surrounded by

God's love and God's Truth while I was working. It's a miracle, really: when I was not with them, they were still exposed to God's ways. In hindsight, I can see that God knew this separation between me and my two youngest children would happen. Thank you, Lord, for making a way for my children to be in private Christian school during that time. If they had been in a public school system when the custody battle had arisen, they would have had even less foundational support! The Bible clearly states in Proverbs 22:6, "Train up a child in the way he should go, and when he is old, he will not depart from it." And this is my hope—a promise from God I hold onto: that my children will heal and return to a positive relationship with God.

One reason why I wrote this book was for the healing of my children and my grandchildren, along with the unlimited amount of people around the world who read this. People need to understand that this process of purging negative energy—emotion—is not always easy. I have been working on this purging process for years now, and it's made a huge difference in my life and in how I show up. My goal is to share what I've learned to expedite your healing process.

It's important to understand the difference between counseling/therapy work and coaching, or even mentoring. Each is unique and has a specific purpose and place in our lives. Counseling/therapy work is helpful when there has been trauma, abuse, addiction, and mental health concerns in your life. Counseling often focuses on past experiences, moving into those experiences with the goal of healing so you can embrace the present. There are various methods of counseling/therapy out there. Personal/executive coaching, on the other hand, embraces where you are today and helps you tap into your potential so you can attain your goals in the future. Coaching is a special bond that's created to extract from you the answers within you, in turn finding your Truth and values, clarifying your dreams and goals, and developing a plan to achieve them.

Mentoring, meanwhile, is a relationship with someone who is sharing their past experiences and lessons and guiding you through their experiences. I offer all of these services, although I am notably not a licensed therapist; I do, however, hold a certificate in Biblical Counseling, as well as Critical Incident Stress (Trauma) Debriefing. As a huge advocate of counseling/therapy, personal/executive coaching, and mentoring, I see the immense power these things hold: by taking a holistic approach in coaching (as all areas of our lives overlap), we can embrace our physical, emotional, relational, intellectual, and career/business goals and the challenging, financial, and spiritual aspects of our lives. In this way, we can expand your leadership capacity and, in turn, your company's growth capacity and profits. You can find out more about this on my website (www.candacemae.com).

CHAPTER 8:
HEALING PERSPECTIVES

NOW, IF YOUR EMOTIONS ARE extremely difficult, you may need help with addressing the immediate situation. If this is the case, by all means, seek help from your doctor—but to get to the core of the matter, you also really need the help of your Creator. Your Creator (God) knows exactly how He designed you, and so God alone knows exactly how to heal you. You must decide to embrace God, for He will heal you, provided you are compliant with your responsibilities.

For those who recognize Jesus Christ as their Lord and Savior and ask His Spirit to reside in their hearts, God will transform their minds and shape them into new creatures.

This means that anyone who belongs to Christ has become a new person. The old life is gone; a new life has begun!
—2 Corinthians 5:17

Accordingly, God will change your DNA, restructure the synapses in your brain, and create new patterns of thought. He does this from the inside as you read His Word (the Bible), meditate on its meaning, and apply it to your life. Through this action, you gain a higher level of awareness and see your thoughts shift, your limited beliefs being replaced with God's Truth and abundance. This is a beautiful process of growth and change. You do not need to fear growth in God: we do, however, hold a healthy fear of God out of awe of His power and respect. Know, though, that God has your best and eternal interests at heart.

This transformation will take time, depending on your level of cooperation: God uses life's circumstances as opportunities to shape you and expand our perspective. God will move you out of your base, animalistic natures and desires and into a higher spiritual focus. As you practice His wisdom given to you through His Spirit and His Word, your faith will grow stronger. As you see Him provide for you and as you share your experiences with others (especially other believers), you will experience oneness with other authentic disciples of Jesus Christ, and you will begin to see the world and people through God's eyes; your experiences will be stronger and more sensitive as the love of God resides deep within you.

Then, by constantly using your faith, the life of Christ will be released deep inside you, and the resting place of his love will become the very source and root of your life. Then, you will be empowered to discover what every holy one experiences—the great magnitude of the astonishing love of Christ in all of its dimensions. How deeply intimate and far-reaching is his love! How enduring and inclusive it is!

Endless love beyond measurement that transcends our understanding—this extravagant love pours into you until you are filled to overflowing with the fullness of God!
—Ephesians 3:17-19

During this process, you will begin to see that you are not alone and that with every experience you face, Christ is experiencing it right there with you through His Holy Spirit, which resides within you. Your awareness grows through each experience as you learn to lean on His wisdom. In this way, you are spiritually reborn, activating the Spirit of God in you so you can begin to live life through spiritual faith, whose resources are from another realm.

So, are you ready to take the ride? I am! I am willing; I am excited. I have known since I was a young girl that I was here to heal my family. It was because of this inner conviction that I knew I had to move away from my family at nineteen so I could become the best person I could be, as fast as possible. Time moves quickly, and with so much growth needed, I didn't have time to waste! My goal was to become my best self; to grow into my God-given potential. I accepted the Lord as a young child in elementary school, at summer Vacation Bible School (VBS). Being so young, I didn't fully know what that meant (to accept the Lord into my heart), so I rededicated my life to God several times through my youth and teenage years, constantly asking God to heal my emotions and bring new life and love into me. It didn't feel like He granted my prayers fast enough: I wanted an immediate transformation. Indeed, wanting—even demanding—immediate results is unfortunately somewhat of a running theme in our society.

While I didn't experience an immediate and radical transformation, I *did* have some powerful experiences with the Lord: I remember accepting Christ into my life in junior high, right around the time of my parents' separation. I started attending a new, powerful, inter-denominational church with my middle sister (she's five years older than me). I could feel God's presence there: His love was like a warm blanket surrounding me, and I couldn't spend enough time with those people. They were so loving, extremely kind, and super supportive. It was amazing.

My love for God was immeasurable; I even had Christian girlfriends that attended my school, and we would study the Bible together. I felt so blessed. Wanting our mother to have this relationship with God and to feel this love encircle her, my sister and I invited her to our church. It was a Spirit-filled church, holding both water baptisms and baptisms in the Spirit, resulting in believers who spoke in tongues. Our mother was afraid and enquired about what we were doing in that church. She could see positive changes in me but didn't understand what was happening. I had grown up in a Wesley Methodist Church that practiced baptism as a child (more like a baby dedication), rather than a full-immersion water baptism as a proclamation of your new faith in Christ (symbolizing your old life being washed away and your being born again through Christ, the water being the embryo's sac fluid). Mom was afraid our new church may be a cult. Perhaps she felt God's love but the feeling was so foreign to her that it scared her. It's a known fact that people will forego what they want in favor of holding onto something that they *don't* want, simply because it's familiar. Think about that: for most people, the unknown is harder to deal with than the misery they are in!

Our mom couldn't understand the spirit of love that permeated the church. Hence, she thought it could be evil. She forbade me from going to the church with my sister. My sister Dee was over eighteen, so our mother couldn't stop her, but I was only thirteen or fourteen, so she had more control over me. I was so deeply hurt. How could she reject such a good thing? I searched my Bible to understand how to handle this. God was real to me; His word was real to me. What He showed me was Ephesians 6:2-3: "Children, obey your parents in the

Lord, for this is right. 'Honor your father and mother'—which is the first commandment with a promise—so that it may go well with you and that you may enjoy long life on the earth."

I wanted to be with the Lord and enjoy His presence daily, but my mother said no. I struggled to understand what to do; after all, God couldn't genuinely want me to turn my back on Him, could he?

I prayed diligently for guidance for days. Finally, I walked to the basement with my Bible in hand, where my mother was doing laundry. I told her directly, "I love God and He loves me. I want to attend that church and grow stronger in the Lord there." She said no; she wanted a "normal" daughter. I replied, "I was afraid you'd say that. I have prayed about this to a great extent and searched my Bible for how to respond. I will honor your wish to be a 'normal girl', as I am still young and living under your roof. I will be the normal you want, and I have asked God to protect me and keep me safe, to bring me back to Him as quickly as He can, and to keep me safe as I obey my mother's request."

God honored that prayer—although I, unfortunately, never went back to that beautiful group of people. I became, instead, a "normal" girl in high school: I experimented with some basic drugs (marijuana; acid; opium) and I got an older boyfriend (who allowed me to experiment but also sheltered me to some degree). The Lord, however, never left me throughout these times.

High school was a defining growth period for me, as it probably is for most of us. It was during my senior year (1980-1981), eighteen months after I took that three-week trip to England with The Warren Youth Chorale, that it became very clear that I wanted more for my life. God blessed me with some great teachers who prompted me to think independently; to reflect on my life thus far; to figure out my purpose; my "why".

Mr. Hayes and Mr. Gordon taught psychology and history in my senior year. They were friends, and they really challenged students to become people of integrity; to understand their own worth and the power they had over their own lives; to understand how they could speak life into the lives of others. They taught us about choices and how our choices would define us. They asked their students to write out answers to the question, *What will your life look like in five/ten years?* Wow, imagine thinking about that at such a young age!

I also had a ninth-grade teacher, Mr. Carter, who was instrumental in this area, as well: Mr. Carter assigned our history class a project, where we were given an annual salary (minimum wage) and had to create a budget to live on. We were forced to keep a smoking habit (the cost of cigarettes being that of a pack a day) in our budget. Then, we had to plan financially how we would move out of our parents' home. In the budget, we had to include the first and last month's rent, our new furniture (cutting out pictures and costs of the furniture we wanted), groceries, utilities, etc. It was an aggravating project. Many of us didn't want to smoke because we wanted to use the money for other things, but that was not an option: he made us keep the expense of cigarettes in the budget. It certainly made us reflect on priorities and consequences, and, above all, on the fact that *we have choices.* If we wanted things in life, we would have to make choices—and smoking is an expensive habit. If we got addicted to cigarettes, the addiction would take away our choices. Similarly, the furniture we liked was not necessarily what we could afford. Now *that* was eye-opening!

It was during my senior year that I realized I wanted to move away from Michigan and my childhood family, as I didn't see any other way to break free. I was being smothered by them: they held the ability to pressure me; to guilt-trip me into making decisions that I did not want to make. If there was something that I valued and wanted, I would have no support in achieving it; instead, I would have to make it happen on my own. I know intellectually this may not be true—we are not meant to do things alone, as God designed us to be interdependent with others—but this was unfortunately not a message I grew up with.

I felt I had to make it happen; I had to get myself into an environment where I could grow. So, I would go about it the only way I knew how: by forcing myself into isolation, away from my known perpetrators.

No one was going to help me get there; to my best self: my siblings said I was spoiled when I tried to upgrade myself or my surroundings. I was the youngest of five, and my mother's career as a schoolteacher after my arrival into the family naturally increased our family's resources. This meant life was completely different for me growing up than it had been for my siblings. My siblings therefore felt I was spoiled, since I ended up receiving a lot more material things than they ever did. Yet "spoiled" comes down to perspective: when I compared myself to my friends, I wasn't getting all that much—yet each person has a different perspective. My siblings' perspectives were valid, even though they may have been different from mine. I like to use a beach ball as a visual aid in teaching this concept on perspectives: depending on the angle you are looking at a beach ball, you will see different colors—meaning when asking someone on the other side of the ball to describe the color of the beach ball, they will see different colors than you. So, should you argue that they are wrong when you don't see the colors they report? Indeed, if we turn the ball sideways, we can see the tip that shows where all the colors come together, meaning every person's perspective was accurate *from their point of view*. This is how life works—meaning we don't need to argue with each other over who is "right"! Instead, we simply need to offer our perspective while honoring theirs as also valid.

I learned to be resourceful growing up: I would create opportunities or take on jobs to earn the money I needed to obtain my desires. Examples of my resourcefulness included helping my brother and sister with their paper routes, babysitting for neighbors and church members, and selling garden-fresh vegetables throughout the neighborhood. We didn't have a garden and we lived in the suburbs, so after visiting my Aunt Cora (who lived in the country and had a huge farm-like vegetable garden), I'd gently place the vegetables in my red radio flyer wagon and walk through our neighborhood selling farm-fresh vegetables. I also used my Easy Bake Oven, in which I would bake small cakes and cookies and sell them along with some lemonade in our side yard. I also sold Girl Scout cookies, though that only earned me badges and prestige!

Fond Memories: A Different Perspective on Childhood

Unlike the stories I have shared thus far, I do have fond memories of my childhood. I especially like the memories of the Wilkins Family Fair that my mom, siblings and I would host for our neighborhood. My mom was a great party planner, so her help planning the fair made it the best fair in the neighborhood every year. We made some good money, too!

The fun began with advertising for the fair: the five of us children would dress up in costumes which we created out of old clothes and Halloween costumes stored in our attic to grab our neighbors' attention as we paraded through the neighborhood announcing the Wilkins Family Fair. I dressed up as a clown with huge plastic bare feet, a big red nose, a colorful wig, and a full jumper outfit. I remember we pulled our red radio wagon wearing our costumes through the neighborhood, carrying balloons and passing out flyers, inviting everyone to our fair, which would begin in the next hour.

Mom, in her creativity, made a movie theatre and stage in our garage using a draped curtain in front of a pop-up movie screen, with folding chairs for the audience. We had a board announcing cartoon movie titles and Wendell the Wizard Magic Show times, which kept everyone hanging around for hours! Participants had to pay for each game, movie, magic show, treat, soda, and such. It was a lot of fun. These were fond childhood memories.

Here's a sample line-up of events at the Wilkins Family Fair:

- **Cartoon Movies**: Setting up an 8mm movie projector, mom played the films:
    - *Popeye and Olive Oil*, among other classic cartoons, like
    - *Mickey Mouse*, the original
    - *Donald Duck & Goofy*
    - *Three Stooges* (an American slapstick comedy team active from 1922 until 1970).
- **Magic Show**: Wendell the Wizard, my oldest, redheaded brother, wore his glitzy green stage tuxedo jacket while aweing the audience with magic.
- **Refreshments**: We used my toys—a cotton candy machine, Easy Bake Oven, and a popcorn machine—to bake delicious cookies and cakes, which we sold to the attendees to enjoy during the movies, as well as soda, lemonade, and hot chocolate.
- Fun carnival games:
    - Clown Toss (a piece of wood with a holey clown face, the aim being to throw beanbags through the clown's eyes (holes) and mouth (another hole)).
    - Rubber Duckies (the rubber ducks had numbers written on their bottom, and they floated in a tub of

water; the goal was to catch a duck using a net and receive a predetermined prize with the correlating number).
- ○ Apples on a String (a string was tied to the apple stem and hung from the ceiling; the participants had their hands tied behind their back and tried to bite their assigned swinging apple).

There were many other activities, too, and we were each assigned with the task of managing one game booth. This taught us event planning, collaboration, marketing, sales, and customer service skills!

Years later, when I was in high school, I saw a sign that someone was having a fair while walking through the neighborhood. Recalling our family fairs, I was excited to attend—but upon walking up to the event, I was sorely disappointed: their fair consisted of a board poker game! I couldn't believe it. This made me realize how special my mom and the memories she had created for us were. I wish she were alive now so I could thank her for all she did. She wasn't perfect—none of us are—but she did the best she could, and she succeeded in creating some fond memories for us. Now, it's my job to hold onto those fond memories as if each memory were a beautiful pearl.

God's Great Design: The Law of Vibration

So, let me stop a moment and explain God's great design before you begin to think that I am tiptoeing into new-age thinking: God is the Creator and Designer of the universe; of this world; of nature, animals, and humanity. Everything around us was ultimately created by God, and in His design, he created laws to keep things running smoothly: just as He created our bodies to function without us consciously thinking about breathing, digesting, or our functioning organs, God created laws like gravity to keep the world and universe operating smoothly each day. We know the sun will rise and set; we know that gravity and the moon cycle control the tides of the oceans. According to lawsoftheuniverse.weebly.com, the Law of Vibration is defined as follows: "Everything in the Universe moves, vibrates and travels in circular patterns. The same principles of vibration in the physical world apply to our thoughts, feelings, desires and wills in the Etheric world. Each sound, thing, and even thought has its own vibrational frequency, unique unto itself."

This aligns with Philippians 4:8, which tells us we should think about all the good things that have happened to us, since when we think of good things, there is no room for fear or doubt. When we have faith to believe in things hoped for but not yet seen, God's Law of Vibration assures us that it will be drawn to us. This is like the phrase "birds of a feather flock together": when things or people share the same frequency of vibration in their thoughts and emotions, much like the frequency of a radio station, things of the same frequency of vibration will find one another.

Now faith is the conviction concerning those things that are in hope, as if it were these things in action, and the revelation of those things that are unseen.
—Hebrews 11:1

Please don't miss this: What God meant for good, Satan uses for evil. While we were designed to be in companionship with God, living in the innocence and purity of love and abundance, as a result of the Great Fall, we lost connection to God and our innocence. Our nature and default thought structures were replaced with Satan's Innate Nature (sin). Therefore, our default thoughts are negative, rebellious, and self-centered. The Law of Vibration still works as God designed it: to draw to us the things we think about in abundance. Thus, when we subconsciously have negative thoughts, the frequency of those thoughts magnifies and pulls similar thoughts to us, in turn creating more pain, deficiency, and evil in the world.

We are fabulously made. It's truly clear there is a Master Designer and Creator of this universe. It boggles my mind to see His majestic powers and to realize that my Creator put a seed of himself within me. I am made of God's seed, and so are you!

CHAPTER 9:
CHOICES: HOW TO OVERCOME

S PEAKING OF SEEDS, WHAT HAPPENS with the seed of a plant? It can sit dormant for thousands of years with nothing happening to it, and it can also be nurtured with nutrient-rich soil and water and grow into a plant, causing life to burst forth from the dead-looking seed.

Notice I said seeds require nutrient-rich soil and water: if the seed is planted in an unsuitable environment, it will most likely not grow at all—or if it does, it may never produce fruit. Why? Because there simply wasn't enough nutrition to support the fruit.

The moral of our story here? Environment matters. Our environments make a *huge* difference in the output of our lives. However, the environment alone is not the only factor impacting our lives: remember, we have choices concerning how we respond to our environments.

If our environments are not conducive to our growth, most of us can choose a new environment, although it can be harder for some to make that decision than others. You might think that everyone can choose what environment they're in, too, but that's not true, either.

In light of the horrors that still pervade this world, we must check in on one another: we must be our brother's keeper, be certain the people around us are safe, and should not be sorry for checking in on someone to let them know we love them or that we haven't heard from them in a while.

Since you are a spiritual being, you may feel something in your spirit (intuition) that guides you to call or visit someone. Follow that! We need each other. Remember, no one is an island, though some of us isolate ourselves and push others away as a knee-jerk reaction to protect ourselves from further pain. We get hurt, isolate ourselves, and eventually numb our sense of needing others. This is a natural sequence of events, and we must guard against it, as it's unhealthy. As Dr. Henry Cloud states in his book *How People Grow*, "People's most basic need in life is relationship. People connected to other people thrive and grow, and those not connected wither and die. It's a medical fact, for example, that from infancy to old age, health depends on the amount of social connection people have."

He has lost connection with the Head, from whom the whole body, supported and held together by its ligaments and sinews, grows as God causes it to grow.
—Colossians 2:19

Even the Bible tells us that we are supposed to connect with and support one another, since we are part of the same body. When Christ's Spirit comes to dwell in us, we become Christ's body manifested on Earth and receive wisdom from Christ's Spirit to guide us as one.

Regardless, our response still seems to be withdrawal when we need each other the most. I recall that when I was hurting in my twenties after I had moved to California, had no food, and was living paycheck-to-paycheck (without enough money to last the two weeks before I'd receive my next paycheck!), I withdrew: I did not want to phone my mother or family back in Michigan. I had that old program my brother instilled in me: *Do not let anyone know you're hurting. They will kick you when you're down and make it worse.* Yet if we don't share our pain or needs with those we love and trust, how can they serve us and help to meet a need they know nothing about?

Again, this example demonstrates the fact that *we are controlled by the programs that are in our subconscious.* Hence, it's our responsibility to become aware of those hidden programs/unconscious beliefs so that we can look deeper into the things we are unbeknownst assuming. Doing this further investigation of our thoughts (or parenting our thoughts) will help us to identify those hidden beliefs so we can validate or replace them.

Embrace moments of frustration by stopping and being thankful for your frustration, since it is indicating to you that there is something out of alignment and that a subconscious belief is being triggered, much like the engine light on the dashboard of our car: it turns on to tell us something is not working properly and needs attention. It's our responsibility in those moments of frustration to parent our thoughts so we can invalidate the underlying assumption/belief that no longer serves us. The frustration you're experiencing is your sign to take responsibility and figure out your underlying assumptions and what beliefs are controlling you. Take those revealed assumptions and compare those beliefs to God's Truth. You may be believing a lie, so make it your mission to toss out the old, false beliefs and replace them with God's Truth. This is how we transform our minds and begin to live a freer life; this is the process of parenting our thoughts; this is how God's Word transforms our minds.

In school, I learned that facts were truths and couldn't be proven wrong. Did you learn that, too? Yet science keeps documenting new truths that make our facts-of-the-present-moment ineffective. Hence, it seems only the truths from our Creator are real *Truth*. Our current conditions and scientific findings may be facts *as of right now*, but facts can be consequences, meaning when circumstances change, outcomes change.

Become aware of your beliefs and stop letting your subconscious beliefs rule your life. You are a spiritual being more powerful than the computerized brain you were gifted with. You get to choose what you believe in, and you get to design your life—and you either do this subconsciously, in the sin-nature default mode, or you can be awakened to God's Truths and accordingly choose God's Truth as your beliefs instead of inheriting those of this world. Think on all things positive, drawing abundance to you, and live your life by His Design through the new nature of Christ's Holy Spirit's power that dwells within you.

When you arrived in this world as a mere four- to ten-pound baby, you were totally dependent on the environment and those around you: you accepted everything and had no choice but to absorb the "truths" and "facts" you heard and saw around you, even during conception in your mother's womb. (This is exactly why God muted Joseph when Mary became pregnant by the Spirit as a virgin: to prevent Joseph's disbelief or doubt from impacting Christ during his development during pregnancy.) People do what people see; they become a product of their environments. Up until the age of seven, our minds are as absorbent as sponges, taking in everything around us so that these stimuli can become the foundational programs that our lives will be lived upon. It is therefore our responsibility (when we become of an accountable age) to subject those beliefs/programs to the scrutiny of our Creator; that we sift through and reprogram our foundational beliefs so that we are working with God's Truth and on the behalf of God to restore this fallen world to relationship with Him.

I was born into much hatred, loneliness, dysfunction, and brokenness, and I was aware of that—yet I was determined to become my best self; the person that God designed me to be. I instinctively knew I had to move away from my family to build the capacity within myself to hold God's Truths. It would be a long journey, and I am still growing every day. I will grow until the day I pass from this world. There is always more to learn; more to be; more to share.

If we grow and hold onto our knowledge without sharing with others, we become like a stagnant body of water, when I want to be like a fresh stream of water, pouring the water of life and God's wisdom into and through others.

Our overriding message here is that we have choices: we can choose to stop and reflect on our lives; we can choose to grow; we can choose to live the life of our dreams. First, though, take this moment to take inventory of where you are and what resources you have to work with, since this will help you to chart the best route for success. Look through your life's history and sift through all the experiences you've had. Get a journal and write down the memories you have, sorting them by good memories and not-so-good memories. Choose to string a beautiful pearl necklace out of all the special moments and memories you've had. If you need help with this, remember I have a free workbook that guides you through numerous exercises to find your gift mix (the unique combination of gifts, talents, traits, strengths, and experiences that makes you, you). You can download a complementary copy of *The You Factor: Your Gift Mix Workbook* at https://giftmix.candacemae.com.

Do you know why I chose a pearl to represent the memories I hold onto? Because pearls are created inside an oyster shell under great pressure and pain, this constant pressure (over a long period) turning the aggressive irritant into a beautiful pearl. A pearl is something we find beautiful and that we cherish, so pick your memories, hold onto the positive outcomes of the bad events, and wear that pearl necklace proudly as a reminder of Philippians 4:8. Keep the learned blessings (the new behavior) and let go of the painful memories from the process.

When you have bad experiences, grieve the pain: feel the sadness, loss, and hurt. Life's circumstances are one way in which God shapes us, so figure out what can be learned through the dark places you have been to and hold onto those lessons. Those lessons are like gold; the buried treasure that you must dig to find which will make you rich with experience, wisdom, and insight; stories that you can share with others to help them learn, too. I call these God Stories.

God Stories are those which were gloomy to live through but yielded something great, presenting a choice regarding what you hold onto. You may have to dig through the rubble of your life to find the gold, but keep digging: it's worth the time spent in discovery! Remember, though, you're not digging into the circumstances or reliving the poor experiences; you're digging through the emotions, releasing the pain, and holding onto the peace and joy that transformed you. You can become bitter or better; it's your choice.

Many people look to public thought leaders who are positive advocates and outspoken teachers and want to be like them—but I wonder if they are willing to do the hard work that those positive thought leaders did to get there. In reality, the majority of those thought leaders have faced difficult, dark days in their lives, and they have worked through them and come out the other side brighter, cleaner, and more hopeful. They know how hard it was, yet they chose to press forward and share their lessons so that others who are stuck in the muck could have hope of getting to the other side. That's what I want for you: I am hoping and praying that as I share my stories, they are helping you get out of your own muck!

The bottom line is *you can follow your dreams*. You are not that negative voice inside your head. You can observe that voice, and because you can observe that voice, you know you are not that voice. Similarly, you are not the emotions that come and go through you. We have already talked about emotions as indicators revealing whether you are on the right path or not, but *you are not the emotions*, so do not let them rule you! Instead, use emotions to enjoy life: when you feel sad, feel sad. Let those feelings flow through you *without* reliving the experiences and stories around the emotions. If you resist letting those feelings flow through you, they will get stuck within your cells, and that is when things begin to stagnate and leave you stuck. So instead, let the emotions flow and share the love that comes; don't hold it in. If you have the thought that you really enjoy talking to a specific person, tell them! If you see something beautiful, say it out loud! Express your positive feelings. If you feel sad, that is also okay to express, although it's best to express your sadness around people you trust. If you are being told not to express yourself, then I suggest you look at the people you are hanging around with (your environment) and examine whether you perhaps have the wrong crowd—or the wrong family! Sometimes, we need to take a break from our families as we regroup and find safe people. Not everyone is a safe person—as we have said, there are predators in this world—and just because someone gave life to another person doesn't mean they're a safe person. Should this be the case for you, *you can rise above the trauma*. Will it be easy? No—but neither is repressing and suppressing the memories and dealing with the constant outbursts your emotions create. Choose your hard. Choosing to embrace and release the pain will be worth it. It's never too late to heal!

Notably, we heal in safe relationships. It's important to realize that we become broken through the relationships around us, and, by the same token, we heal in our *safe* relationships with others.

Above all, remember that it is an honor to be human! I am thrilled with the privilege of having a human experience. I did not always think this way, however: I grew up feeling very lonely, in a home where the words *I love you* were not spoken. I was starving for love. I used to get my hugs from our dog Misty, a gray, mid-sized poodle mix. I used to give her bear hugs, squeezing her so tight my family used to tell me I was hurting her. Maybe I was a bit rough, but I needed those hugs! I used to see Hallmark commercials and cry because the love shown was so touching to me—and painfully pointed out what I lacked. I craved that love, and I wondered why I had never experienced love like that in my family. I still cry watching Hallmark movies! I still crave a healthy, loving relationship founded on growth and truth.

I admit I am a personal growth junkie. I came from a generationally dysfunctional family—though now, I think most of us do!—and from an early age, I felt called to break those generational bonds of dysfunction. I quickly realized, however, that to do so, I would have to heal myself first.

That healing has been a journey, and my children grew up while I was on this journey. They got the best of who I was at each moment, which was not always ideal! Be gentle with yourself throughout the growth process.

I want future generations to be healthier; to see new opportunities; to find better ways to connect and relate. I want the generational lies to be removed; for the Truth to be told and embraced; for the earth and humans to be restored to a full relationship with God. I focus intentionally on personal growth daily, and as a result, I grow profoundly fast. I see people around me from high school that are still stuck in their ways, emotionally stuck during their day-to-day lives. I, however, have also been blessed enough to become a part of several growth-oriented communities that are focused on the preeminence of Jesus Christ, and those communities are rich in love and focused on growth.

While all of this information is critical for the commencement of your growth journey, what I've discovered is that while education brings knowledge, it doesn't necessarily bring transformation: you can read all kinds of self-help books and learn processes, but knowing how to do it in theory and being transformed are two completely different things. Here, I like to use the example of building an airplane: it's possible to know how to build an airplane in theory, but the actual experience of building an airplane and it being successful in flight is a totally different thing. So, while I want future generations to be healthier, I must first experience a transformation myself, not just a want to change; I must not only study change and know "how" people change, but I must also go through the metamorphosis process and experience such change *before* I can help others through their change. It's because people see a change in me that they know I can help *them* change!

Through encounters with Christ's Holy Spirit, I was truly transformed from the inside. The Holy Spirit offers us gifts of knowledge (knowing right from wrong), fortitude (having the strength to stand up and be strong), understanding (enabling us to follow God's path), piety (to worship and pray), counsel (to enlighten and guide us), wisdom (to feel God's presence beside us), and fear of the Lord (to always be awed by the mighty wonders of our God). It's important to realize that it's not what we know that counts, but what we *do* with what we know.

MINISTRY OF THE SPIRIT
(Isaiah 11:2–3 | Ephesians 4:11-17 | Acts 2:42)

1. **Wisdom**
   Ability to think and act using knowledge, experience, understanding, common sense, and insight. Attributes such as unbiased judgment, compassion, experiential self-knowledge, self-transcendence and non-attachment, and virtues such as ethics and benevolence.

2. **Understanding**
   noun: comprehension.
   adjective: sympathetically aware of other people's feelings; tolerant and forgiving.

3. **Knowledge**
   facts, information, and skills acquired by a person through experience or education.

4. **Counsel** (advice)

5. **Fortitude**
   Strength of mind that enables a person to encounter danger or bear pain or adversity with courage.

6. **Piety**
   Devotion and reverence to religious practices and God.

7. **Fear of the Lord**.
   To be in awe of his holiness, to give him complete reverence, and to honor him as the **God** of great glory, majesty, purity, and power.

So, what are you doing with your knowledge and education? I know a woman who is very experienced with helping the handicapped and emotionally challenged and she knows what to do when working with others, but when it comes to her own life and that of her daughter, she is completely adrift concerning how to interact or how her own behaviors are being perceived. Why is that?

Simply, the programs/beliefs she grew up with are still the strongholds in her subconscious mind: they limit what she sees and experiences in her own life, which is amazing (though sad) to observe. We talked just the other day, and she told me about what she does for work; then, later in the conversation, she described the interpersonal dynamics of what was going on in her life between her and her grown daughter. It was so interesting to hear the paradox of what she was saying she did for work and her behavior with her daughter. She could not see the fact that she was *reacting* to her daughter rather than *responding* in the way she does with those she works with. This is her blind spot, and we all have our own blind spots (things others clearly see in us but we do not). Our blind spots may be good or bad character traits and behavior.

Now, if her daughter knew that her mom treated others differently at work—and she does—she would certainly be hurt—yet this mother feels very betrayed and hurt by her daughter: while the mother says she forgives her daughter, you can hear and see the bitterness she feels. She is still refusing to be the responsible adult and reach out to her daughter for reconciliation: she says that until her daughter states how much she appreciates the sacrifices she made for her, she wants nothing to do with her daughter. Wow! How tragic. For how many years will their relationship continue to be lost?

At the same time, the daughter is holding onto how much her mom has not done for her, and is waiting to receive acknowledgment of all the pain she feels her mother has put her through. Meanwhile, the mother refuses to admit the pain her daughter feels. The mom knows all the sacrifices she made to raise her daughter, and she knows she did the best she could.

This ultimately creates a sad standoff, leading to years going by with no relationship—years that cannot be got back. Both perspectives are true for the person who holds the experience. Both are in an emotional prison, longing to be restored to the other, and this pain and discomfort will create dis-ease within them—and the dis-ease of emotion quickly becomes disease of the body. This is why we need to forgive: so we can be whole and restored to good health.

Validate the feelings of others, even if their perspective is different from yours and you don't believe their perspective is the whole truth, because it is *their* truth in that moment. Validating doesn't mean agreeing; it simply means we understand and honor their perspective and experience. Similarly, it's okay to ask for forgiveness from another who is hurting because of what we did, even though we never intended to hurt them and did the best we could in those circumstances. Asking for forgiveness gives validation to their feelings and makes room to breathe and restore relationships.

We must choose to respond differently from the way we reacted in the past if we want a different outcome. This takes intention and awareness.

Choosing to respond with intention instead of allowing a knee-jerk reaction is an extremely powerful practice in family dynamics and interpersonal relationships: if you think about it, everyone we cross paths with is in an interpersonal relationship with us! This means you have lots of opportunities to practice awareness and responding with intention. Remember, those frustrating moments are something you can rejoice in; they present an opportunity for a moment of self-awareness and choice concerning how to respond. Choose wisely!

Try this exercise: Next time you get triggered, stop yourself from carrying out that instinctive knee-jerk reaction and instead say to the other person, "Wow, I get it. That must be extremely hard. I am sorry you had to go through/are currently going through that." Notice the facial expressions of the other person when you respond: you may notice both shock and appreciation on their face. Suddenly, they feel heard, and they will be thinking (or perhaps will respond with), *Really? You get it? You understand the pain I've been experiencing while I've been trying to figure out this thing called life? You acknowledge the fact that the choices I made were the best choices I could see at that moment in time? You're not judging me?*

This is true! When someone validates my struggles and pain, I suddenly feel like I can breathe for the first time: I can stop trying to prove to them and the world that I'm hurting. Once I feel heard, I can begin to breathe and start to listen to their experience with compassion.

In a nutshell, love heals all things; even the physical growth of a young person who has been traumatically hurt is often stunted when they don't receive a sufficient amount of love. Our entire bodies shut down the production of the energy that would otherwise go into our growth to protect us in these situations, and it is only when we are out of the (perceived) danger that our bodies can then return their energy back to the growth process.

I have observed hindrances to growth for ten years in my loved ones, as well as the moment when they enter a safe period and their growth starts again. Our bodies are amazing! We were wonderfully made.

CHAPTER 10:
A SHORT NOTE ON
THE POWER OF WORDS

WORDS HAVE POWER. WHEN I was a child, there was a saying we would say whenever others insulted us; it was our attempt to diminish the power and pain of the insults they verbally threw at us. The saying was, "Sticks and stones may break my bones, but words will never hurt me." What a lie! Sticks and stones may break our bones, yes—and words will not cause direct physical damage, yes; but words absolutely have the power to hurt us. As a matter of fact, words hurt us at a deeper level than sticks and stones *ever* will. We are first and foremost spiritual beings; our physical bodies are merely the housing in which our spirits reside.

Words are vibrational, and they attack our souls. Hence, it's a great injustice to tell our children that words will never hurt them, since that leaves them vulnerable to attack and hurting from insults without understanding *why* they are hurting so deeply. This creates shame and eats at their self-worth. As a matter of fact, words are so powerful that God spoke the universe into being. Words create. Words can offer hope, peace, and understanding—or they can be words of pain, hurt, condemnation, and rejection. Name-calling can leave deep scars on one's soul!

We must be careful here. I am still learning the power and depth of this truth! The Bible is clear on this topic, as it says our words come from and reveal the conditions of our hearts.

> *But the things that come out of a person's mouth come from the heart, and these defile them.*
> —Matthew 15:18 NIV

When our children, spouses, friends, or coworkers hurt us, we may lash out at them with words of anger and pain, labeling their behavior as we see it by calling them names—or so we tell ourselves.

When you tell someone they are selfish, however, you are reinforcing that behavior and making it a part of their identity, especially if others have said that or similar things to them before. While it is important to bring it to someone's attention if you are unhappy with their behavior, it is *essential* that you are conscious of *how* you bring it up. Identify that their *behavior* is selfish, not that *they* are selfish. This is difficult and takes practice. I still struggle with it myself.

To be clear, we don't want to tell them, "You are selfish." That is making their identity selfish. Rather, consider saying something like, "When you act this way or perform this behavior, I feel as if you do not care about me or others." The latter example is objectively calling out the behavior, not identifying *them* as the negative behavior itself. Do you see and hear the difference? Can you feel the difference between how you receive those two sentences?

Regardless, you have the power to speak life and change into people's lives—or to condemn and break them more. You may not have realized the gravity of that fact up until now, but now that you know your words have power, you have a responsibility to change the words you direct toward others. Instead of labeling their negative behavior as if it is their identity, say instead, "I know you are better than the behavior you are exhibiting right now." See how that resonates with them. In all likelihood, they will become introspective and begin to scrutinize their own behavior productively.

Pay attention to your thoughts and behavior regarding how you relate to others. Start thinking about what you're thinking about. Begin to parent your thoughts. Own your thoughts. Capture them before you speak them. Validate or correct your self-talk. Be gentle with yourself. Remember Philippians 4:8: "... whatever is true, whatever is noble, whatever is right, whatever is pure, whatever is lovely, whatever is admirable..." Think on these things towards yourself as well! Find the good in yourself and others. Speak life into yourself and into others. Will you be the person who builds people up and speaks life into them, or will you be another predator tearing yourself and others down?

Yes, I did say predator—and while that may sound harsh, please don't condemn yourself too much: in all likelihood, you have been a predator with your words, but you are a work in progress. Begin today to be a joy bringer; a peacemaker; a lover of souls. Let your words be positive words of creation.

CHAPTER 11:
THE ABUNDANCE VS
SCARCITY MINDSET

REMEMBER THOSE UNCONSCIOUS BELIEFS AND programs? Most of the time, we are living on autopilot (i.e., running on the beliefs in our subconscious). When in this state, we don't even *think* about our habits; words fly out of our mouths and we don't even hear ourselves. That's why Matthew 15:18 says, "But the words you speak come from the heart—that's what defiles you."

This happened to me very recently, only this time, I was self-aware and caught myself—or should I say it was pointed out to me and *then* I became self-aware! Here's what happened: I was out driving with my adult daughter. We'd just made a trip to the grocery store, and I felt the need to emphasize to her (I suddenly realized I was doing this regularly!) how much money I spent and how fast the money from my savings was being spent supporting the two of us. I was saying that she was going to have to get a job and contribute at some point soon. I was in the process of launching a business (about eighteen months into being an entrepreneur), so what clients I had at that point didn't yet cover all my business and living expenses. I felt taken advantage of as I watched my savings dwindle.

My daughter finally said, "Mom, why do you have to be so *negative?*"

That caught my attention. Negative? Was I being negative? I thought I was practicing abundant thinking!

Then, I realized that having an abundance mindset is much more than just watching the words we speak; rather, an abundance mindset must exude from our very being at an *energetic* level. This was a new level of self-awareness for me. I sincerely pondered the thought: was I being negative? If so, that meant I was not exercising abundant thinking. Negativity comes from a scarcity mindset, not one of abundance!

Oh my! I was, indeed, being negative! I was thinking that there was a scarcity of resources. I was focused on the default mode of *what's in it for me?* and was trying to hold onto what I had in fear that it would run out and not be replaced. Was I subconsciously believing that without a traditional job (i.e., working for someone else) I would not earn a sufficient income? I have great value to share with others, and I have a solid business structure that can earn income through the serving of others—and yet I was not practicing abundant thinking. This was a great insight for me, in real time! I thanked my daughter for that feedback, and she was surprised at my response.

Now that I am aware of the subtlety of this scarcity mindset, I have a choice concerning how I am going to respond. I immediately apologized for creating a sense of low value and lack of safety for her, and I immediately asked God to help me be more mindful of abundance. All my resources are from God, and I need to be consistently grateful! There is enough for me to share, though that doesn't change the fact that as an adult, she has a responsibility to contribute.

Several stories in the Bible tell us how God provides for the needs of His people, one of which being found in 2 Kings 4:1-7 about a widow in great debt: she asked a prophet, Elisha, for help and guidance, and he asked her what she had in her house. She only had a small amount of olive oil. He instructed her to borrow bottles from neighbors and fill them with the oil she had, which she did obediently. Then, she was instructed to go sell the oil, pay her debt, and live on the proceeds. God multiplied what she had. Note that she had to follow the advice, work obediently, and demonstrate faith, and *then* God multiplied her efforts.

I noticed this same pattern on December 9, 2020, when I suddenly had a massive, endgame stroke: at first, I was in denial and was going to go back to bed. Had I gone back to bed, I would not be alive today; either that, or I would be severely physically handicapped. Regardless, I didn't go back to bed because it was as though an angel pushed me, knocking me over, my right side hitting the bathtub. I heard a pop (I broke three ribs and had a collapsed lung) to get my attention! It was obvious as I sat on the floor with my right arm trapped inside the bathtub that I was unable to move my right side—certainly a stroke!

Long story short, I had to use my words to speak life into myself. I claimed the power and dominion granted to me as a daughter of God to be healed through the stripes Jesus bore prior to the cross. I admitted I was helpless and powerless to do anything on my own accord, so while I was submitting to God's will in my life, I asked for clarification concerning what I understood from Him to be my purpose and mission. I stated what I had heard Him ask me to do and reminded Him of my faithfulness in taking action upon what I understood. I reminded Him I was in the middle of a two-week silent retreat focusing on His Spirit and that I'd just signed a personal covenant three days prior dedicating my life and business completely to Him. I specifically cried out that if I understood Him with my purpose, I'd need to have my full health restored: to walk, talk, write, and think so I could do His work. Then, I submitted and waited for His guidance.

Sure enough, He came through and provided miraculous healing for me. If you'd like to hear my testimony and miraculous journey of immediate recovery, please listen to my interview on the All-In podcast on my website (https://candacemae.com/podcast-a-miracle-in-the-middle-of-transition/). As I reflect on God's faithfulness to me, the more my trust in Him grows and the more I follow the Knowing or intuition He has given me. God requires us to verbalize our faith and then step out with action, in obedience and demonstrating our faith. Only then are His miracles done.

Something to note: Remember God's Universal Law of Vibration. Our energy goes before us into a room; people feel our vibes (vibrational energy) even before we speak. If I have negative or critical inner thoughts (which is the default mode as a result of the environment in which I grew up—a result of the "sin" nature), then that negativity will be felt by the people around me. My aura will have a lower frequency of vibration.

As I begin to soften and change within (which happens through the transformation of my mind with the help and guidance of Christ's Holy Spirit), my energy vibration and frequency rises, and changes are made in my DNA. Our DNA has switches that can be turned on or off depending on the frequency of our energy. This is quite amazing to think about! Hence, by challenging my autopilot thinking and changing out those subconscious negative beliefs/programs, I am literally becoming a new person at a DNA level.

Further, as I soften and change within, I begin to attract different people into my life energetically—and the people who are already in my life begin to respond to me differently. Some will fall away because they no longer fit with the person I am growing into or have already become: our vibrational energy is no longer a match, so we naturally drift apart. Further, as I grow, my circumstances also begin to change around me to match the person I am now: the higher vibrational energy will attract like energy.

Do you see the power of staying focused on positive thinking, as Philippians 4:8 instructs us to do? God created us, and He's provided us with guidance and His Holy Spirit to dwell in us, but we must first choose to accept Him and to walk with an intention and self-awareness concerning His Presence.

This explains so much to me, and also means I can be gentle with myself for having so many relationships/marriages. Usually, I date serially and end up in a permanent relationship: marriage. I have been married four times already and reflecting now, I see the progression in the relationships; that is, how I was evolving and growing continuously.

Brian (my late ex-husband) once said to me, "I have never seen anyone grow as fast as you." I never forgot that; I appreciated those words then, and I still do now. I saw a lot of pain in my life, and from my perspective, I literally couldn't grow fast enough. My goal has always been to be my best self; to grow and to help others to grow, paying it forward and healing my family—although we must realize that *not everyone wants to grow with us*. God even tells us that we must always choose Him over others. When we choose God, we are choosing to grow (if we have an authentic disciple relationship).

I have experienced emotional pain and self-judgment in the past, when I heard my children talk about who I was when they were small, and as a result, I had to practice being gentle with myself. I developed this response when someone brought up behavior from my past: "I'm sorry I was not a perfect parent. I did the best I could with what I had at the time. I kept pressing forward to be someone better. Can I get any acknowledgment about who I am today and how far I've grown?" Since I've implemented this response, the subsequent reply has always been positive: they say yes, they see my growth.

It's okay for people to want to hear you apologize for who you were, but it's *not* okay for them to keep rubbing your nose in matters that are behind you—things you cannot change.

Be aware of who you are and who you are becoming. You can grow and grow and grow and become more and more, but what are you doing with that growth? Are you aware of your growth and what you were like before you grew? How are you helping people around you to grow? Are you growing for the sake of growth only? Do you need people to acknowledge your growth? I suppose we all need validation to some degree, but have *you* acknowledged your growth? Self-acknowledgment is critical; it's important to take time to reflect and let your growth catch up with you. You need to refresh your self-image to embrace who you have become; otherwise, your growth will be beyond your self-image, and you cannot outperform your self-image. Hence, reflection and acknowledgment of your growth are absolutely essential. It's crucial to embrace your growth and live out your best self!

I have had several coaches in my life, and I have a journal in which I write notes during and after each coaching session. I recently took out that binder and read through the entries from a year ago. It had bi-monthly updates, and as I read the entries from March 2019, I found I didn't even recognize the person I was reading about! Truly, I had experienced so much growth during that year that I was literally a new person. I had grown immensely, and seeing that growth was powerful.

Years ago, I remember seeing my brother, Lowell, after a ten-year absence. I made a comment about how messed up our family was and the fact that I was tired of them holding me to an image that was no longer accurate. He said to me, "Relax, Candie. Realize people hold onto the image of you from when they last experienced you. You may have grown, but they haven't been around you to see that growth, so what they see of you is what they last experienced."

Now *that's* insightful—and this insight demonstrates how important it is to stay connected with prospects and friends on a somewhat regular basis just so they can be aware of your growth! Send them cards, video chats, or something else periodically. This is the power of social media: people can witness your growth online right in front of them! Be transparent and authentic and people will seek you out.

As you become aware of how you have grown, you will perform accordingly. I had done a ton of growth, but I was not aware of it. I was aware of new breakthroughs happening almost daily, but I wasn't aware of how that was showing up to others.

At one point, my main business coach pointed out to me that I had joined an abundance of classes and growth communities, to the point where I had around sixteen coaches (a bit extreme). My reason for this was that each coach was mentoring me in a different area of my life or aspect of my business. The topics overlap at times, but it was all still assisting me in transforming my thoughts and beliefs so I could grow abundantly, both personally and professionally. I don't recommend this many coaches for any one person, however! Nonetheless, at the beginning of me launching my business, it was important for me to jumpstart it—and now, the value of my ongoing mentors and coaches lies in their helping me prioritize, maintain, and scale my business. Indeed, I have found that by far the best way to do that is to hire coaches and mentors who can get me there faster, since I can learn from their tried-and-true experiences. It's also helpful to join powerful growth-oriented communities. I looked at all my learning as if I were back in college, multiple classes all working together toward a higher degree.

I stand by the fact that there is value in having one voice in your life—but I also believe that one voice doesn't have to be limited to one person; it does, however, need to be one *message*. Everything needs to be working together in the same direction. If all the voices are giving the same message, you may hear things said in different ways by the different people, with different experiences, which ultimately leads to an "Aha!" moment that you otherwise may miss. Hearing the same message in different words means a higher likelihood of it deeply resonating.

I have found that different mentors fulfill different needs: for one, it was important for me to find female mentors, since women have different perspectives and life experiences to men. Second, I found that the mentors I was drawn to all happened to have their own tribe, each with their own lingo (meaning staying in just one tribe alone really limits your vocabulary). I also noticed that some mentors wanted their tribe to think that this was the only way of doing things, when in actuality, being exposed to many mentors has enabled me to see multiple patterns of success and identify which work best for me. Third, I enjoy working with a diverse group of business owners with different modalities (i.e., different methods, goals, and visions). Finding the best method for you and laser-focusing is key to quick results.

The bottom line is, we all need mentors and coaches. As I reflect on my mom, I recall her saying to me when I voiced my want for the one-to-one tutoring she'd provided my brother with, "You are smart and capable. You can figure it out on your own." The thing is, though, I *wanted* help; I didn't *want* to figure it out alone. I wanted to learn faster than I could on my own, and I wanted a relationship nurtured by all the attention my brother was getting daily! I wanted to be tutored like she was doing with my brother, and I wanted her to assure me I was on the right course. I wanted a bit of time with total focus on me! Essentially, I wanted a partner to help me; to talk with me and be a sounding board; to help to guide me onto the right track. Heck, I *still* yearn for that! That's why I ultimately hired a coach, and that's why I pay for consultants and hire staff to help me.

If you're anything like me, you understand that time is precious and we're not guaranteed tomorrow—meaning that the urgency of growing and expanding our potential, businesses, and those around us is essential. So, if you understand the value of having a coach speak life into you and believing in you when you don't believe in yourself, guiding you to get to a high level of achievement faster than you would on your own, I'd *love* to connect with you. I offer a free consultation for those interested in exploring this avenue. This merely presents an opportunity for us to get to know each other and establish whether we'd be a good fit and for me to provide you with one actionable tip you can implement immediately. If interested, you can book a call from my website (www.candacemae.com/schedule-an-appointment).

Do you know what you value? Have you gone through a values exercise? I have a great exercise listed in Chapter 6 of your companion workbook that will walk you through discovering, prioritizing, and aligning your values. If you've not done this yet, please take a moment now to make a list of your values and to whittle them down via the process of elimination: pick the top ten values that mean the most to you and then narrow those ten values down to your top five values. Does your life reflect those values in your day-to-day activities? If they don't, perhaps they are not truly your values—or if they are, you are clearly out of alignment with them and are not living according to your values.

Do you know what you value most right now? Look at your checkbook and the appointments on your calendar: where are you spending your money and time? If your family is extremely valuable to you, are you showing that by actually blocking out periods to be with them? I am guilty of not practicing what I preach in this respect occasionally; however, I recognize that it is only through intentional planning that I can design my life and carve out time to spend with my grown children, and grandchildren. Try making events with your family a priority, just like you do with work events. Get into the habit of putting your family time on your calendar first and *then* fitting your work events around family. My oldest daughter is particularly good at keeping her family as her highest value!

As with the other chapters thus far, please take this moment to refer to your companion guide and complete the exercises, which are designed to help you to initiate/continue your own personal growth. It is so important that you take the time to pause and reflect on your thoughts; to parent your thoughts. Practice reframing when you observe negative or limiting thoughts. Challenge your beliefs. Be sure your beliefs line up with your values. Again, take a moment to acknowledge, absorb, and make peace with all of your incoming thoughts and feelings. Let your feelings guide you to higher levels of vibration. If you're feeling sad or down, those are lower vibrations. Practice letting the emotion flow so you can move into higher levels of peace, joy, and love.

CHAPTER 12:
LIVE WITH INTENTION
AND URGENCY

TIME IS OUR MOST PRECIOUS asset. We only have the present moment. We are not guaranteed even one moment more of life beyond the present moment. I know that all too well now: when I had that massive left ICA stroke, the doctors claimed it was an endgame stroke—and yet I am blessed enough to say that God worked a physical, emotional, and spiritual miracle in my life and restored my health.

Think about this for a moment: When someone has a stroke or a heart attack, their body doesn't announce to them that they are going to be hospitalized today; it just happens in the spur of the moment. So, embrace this moment for all it is! Stop squandering the time away.

Design your life; take time to pause from your busy schedule to meditate and connect with God and your inner self; practice being in the present moment. Each moment in focused meditation transforms your mind. You do not realize the power those moments of clarity and quietness of mind have. During these moments, God is connecting with you and feeding your soul—and when we tune into a higher frequency through meditation, we find love and peace, or the essence of God, within us. This replaces doubts and fears and instills strength, fortitude, peace, and joy that overflows so we are able to serve others from the abundance that overflows.

The ideas you receive during these quiet moments are downloads from God. Have you ever thought of ideas in that way? If so, this is because ideas come from our higher selves; from a spiritual realm. I believe all the resources we need to make our ideas a reality will be provided to us when we're connected to God through a relationship with Him. He is the Creator of all things, and if He provides you with an idea, I believe He will also provide you with the means to make it come to fruition. Again, we need to stay connected to God's presence through awareness and develop the vibrational mindset of abundance. Refer to the chapter where we briefly discussed the Law of Vibration for a refresher on the fact that the abundance mindset must be authentic throughout your body's vibration. Getting cool ideas is great, but what you *do* with those ideas is what counts. The longer we wait to act upon the ideas we receive, the likelier we are to let the idea die. The universe likes speed.

Remember, transformation is an internal journey. What a life we have here on Earth, and what a journey our lives are! I truly believe it is our responsibility to stay close to our Creator and to focus on our growth every single day—especially through those difficult times. Indeed, focusing on growth during hard times is certain to help you to rise above the pain, as doing so gives meaning and purpose to the pain.

The secret is your mindset: growth can be found in what was previously thought to be repressive circumstances.

In nature, we consistently find beautiful things that develop through pressure, friction, heat, and struggle—a metaphor for our lives, since our struggles are ultimately key for our spiritual growth. God uses our circumstances to grow and stretch us and develop our faith. Our inner beauty and mature spiritual living evolve from the process of growing through the process of pain. After all, how does the caterpillar turn into a beautiful butterfly? It must go through the cocoon stage—a death and rebirth process! For the butterfly to be strong enough to live and fly, it must go through a struggle to break out of the cocoon. If you or I were to peel open the cocoon to stop the struggle, the emerging "butterfly" would not have wings strong enough to fly. Without allowing the butterfly the opportunity to develop the strength of its wings through struggle, it will die, unable to fly—much like us and our children! In this way, if *we* face no problems or someone constantly rescues us, we can never develop the fortitude and strength to navigate our own lives.

Indeed, nature has many of these beautiful lessons for us: birds teach their babies to fly by making them jump out of a nest up to fifty feet in the air, for example. Those birds will certainly die if they hit the ground, but the parents are nearby, watching, guiding, and encouraging them all the way. The parents cannot coddle the baby birds' fears and let them stay in the nest, since if the baby birds don't learn to fly, they will be killed in the nest by predators—and so the baby birds must take the leap. If a baby bird refuses to take the leap, the mother bird will bring briars and thorns into the middle of the nest, forcing the baby to the edges of the nest so they can avoid the pain—and if the baby still refuses to take the leap, the mother bird will nudge the baby out of the nest altogether, forcing it to fly.

We, too, must face our fears if we want to learn to soar. We can go through this life on autopilot, not exploring our purpose and working a job we hate to pay the bills; we can tolerate existing rather than thriving during our existence because our fears and limiting beliefs hold us back too much. Or—as I encourage you to do!—you can dream—and not only that, but step *into* your dreams with actionable steps. Begin to be aware of your thoughts, and you'll be surprised by the amount of negative self-talk that is in your subconscious. Become aware of those thoughts, pull up those programs in your subconscious, and examine your hidden beliefs. Replace the beliefs that are no longer serving you. Parent your thoughts daily: observe, guide, and direct them, just like you would guide and direct children.

How do you do that? Ask yourself, *What are the assumptions behind the decisions I make?* When you hear yourself say, "I can't do that," ask yourself, *Why can't I do that? What is stopping me?* When you hear your answer, ask yourself, *Is that really true? Who told me that?* You may be surprised by your answers! Then, ask yourself, *Is that true, or is that merely a fact of the past? I am not my past. My past does not determine my future.* Find out what God has to say about your identity and who you are and understand how He created you. Embrace His beautiful Truth of who you are, and the power, authority, and dominion He has given you. I myself would love to work with you as you progress through this journey, so if you're someone who desires to grow faster than you can alone, and if the messages you have read in this book have resonated with you, reach out for a free exploratory strategy session with me. You've got nothing to lose and everything to gain!

I look forward to connecting with you. Again, you can schedule an appointment through my website at www.candacemae.com/schedule-an-appointment.

Here's a declaration of strength and identity I like to use. Feel free to adopt this for yourself if it pleases you; just adjust the pronouns as they fit for you!

I am a woman of God redeemed by Jesus Christ. I am loved. I am beautiful. I am valuable. I am chosen. I am safe and secure in Him. I am forgiven and no longer bound by the past. I am dead to sin but alive in Jesus Christ. I have been clothed in His righteousness. I am strong in the Lord and empowered by His Spirit. I am fully equipped to run the race and fight the battle ahead. I choose to put on the whole armor of God and stand firm in the Truth. I boldly take up the shield of faith which can extinguish the fiery darts of the enemy. I will put on the helmet of salvation to protect my mind. I will take up the sword of the Spirit, the Word of God, as my defense. I will hide His Word in my heart. I will be joyful and give thanks to God. I will pray continually and keep watch for my Savior. I will abide in His love now and forevermore.

What I like about having an integrated life is that I can pull from all areas of my life and enrich my life accordingly: if I go on a business trip, I can take my partner or friend with me or meet a friend at the destination. I can buy myself an outfit or a gift on that same business trip to remind myself of the trip, and I can get my exercise in while having a family member or friend join me on a walk or bike ride so I am integrating social and emotional bonding with physical fitness. The overarching message here? Live big! Live rich!

Living a rich, abundant life includes many areas of your life, including having dynamic, well-rounded friendships, strong familial relationships, romance in your marriage, financial stability, good health via proper nutrition and exercise, being active in philanthropic causes that help others, animals, or our planet, and having hobbies that allow you to destress and pursue something fun, as well as working in a business or industry that adds value to our lives. These things create a rich life. Our emotional development, our spiritual development, and giving back to our community are all equally pivotal.

Remember, *values are caught more than they are taught*—so by doing philanthropic activities (perhaps with family or friends), you create great memories while modeling the importance of giving back and helping others instead of only focusing on your own needs and just having fun. Some families spend a lot of time in Disneyland, fairgrounds, and community events—which create great family memories but don't give back to society. Such activities alone are not sufficient for teaching our children about the importance of giving back; they do, however, teach them to have fun and perhaps quality time with others *and* to focus on their own wants. Of course, fun activities are super important, but be sure to balance them with examples of community involvement. All work and no play isn't healthy, nor is all play and no work! It's all about harmonizing and living a balanced or integrated life. It takes daily intentionality to keep our lives in a healthy rhythm and harmony.

CHAPTER 13:
RESOURCES AND WAYS TO
SPEAK LIFE INTO OTHERS

D O YOU TRULY BELIEVE THAT most people are doing the best that they can? Do you believe that even when somebody personally hurts others, they may still be acting to the best of their ability at that time? Taking a moment to look past a person's hurtful words and behavior to understand the pain they are in during that moment will change the way you see the world and how you interact with others. It's not easy, but it's helpful.

If we can understand that each person is doing the best that they can at any given moment, the way we see the world can change. I am not saying that we need to be accepting and approve of others' misbehavior; rather, I am saying that while bad behavior needs to be addressed, it's important to realize that each person is more than their behavior. How we respond to their pain (rather than to their bad behavior alone) is essential when we are looking to create positive change in the world.

Consequences are important, yet it's still important to realize that *people are not their behavior.* People act out—that's their behavior— but their behavior is not who they are. People who have been deeply wounded often have high reptilian brain functioning, in the sense that they are constantly living in a state of fear, sometimes for years on end. This is overwhelming and naturally leads to skepticism, which in itself leads to heightened reactions and defensiveness. They become hypersensitive and over-reactive.

I can't imagine living through the pain that so many people face daily—and many of these people ultimately turn to substance abuse to cope with such pain. This is something I have witnessed firsthand: someone dear to me became addicted to drugs and alcohol, and their behavior become abusive and toxic. I could not allow this person to keep living with me. This decision was hard, but boundaries and consequences needed to be established.

This loved one drifted for four years. Time passed very quickly, and their possessions were slowly either lost or stolen. They watched high school friends obtain steady jobs and start to build their careers while they remained stuck, controlled by their substances. Jobs would be obtained and lost, since they were not stable or reliable enough to keep them. They grew weary as they noticed some friends finish college or enter marriage and have children. Angry outbursts would occur concerning the fact that everyone was moving forward while they were regressing—as if they were a victim. Perhaps they were, trapped by their addictions and unable to take responsibility for their life. They were in constant struggle: they had surrendered their ability to think and choose, and instead were living on autopilot, letting their anger build all the while.

After couch-surfing with family and friends, they began to live in their car. They enrolled in recovery programs multiple times, but were ultimately unable to stick with the program: their emotional pain was controlling their behavior. Upset and filled with pain and shame, they found themselves unable to share with the program staff the fact that they were experiencing flashbacks of prior life events; instead, they would lock themselves in the bathroom—or, worse, leave the premises. The program staff were understandably unable to understand what was happening and would kick them out of the program, once again confirming their unconscious belief that no one understood them or cared enough to support their needs.

Those on the outside (myself included) could not understand what was happening, either; it was a vicious cycle of them obtaining a stable job and then something happening that would emotionally set them off, throwing them off-balance. This would produce a knee-jerk reaction, and things would spiral out of control, depression, lack of ability to control sleep patterns, and suicidal ideations setting in. Getting into a regular routine is difficult for those who suffer from anxiety, depression, and addiction, yet a structured routine is often exactly what is needed.

However, love conquers all. With a lot of prayers, they ended up on my doorstep about a month before the global pandemic lockdown commenced, and I was grateful to have my loved one with me, where I knew they were safe. The initial few weeks were hard, but after receiving a loving response from me, their emotions settled as they felt more acceptance and safety. When I began to acknowledge their pain and how difficult that past few years must have been for them, feelings of validation and love started to set in, and when I repeatedly said, "I love you and I'm glad you're here with me," their heart softened—not the first time I said it, but through repetitive reinforcement. I was truly glad my loved one was safe with me, and when I shared that I wished their life experiences could have been different, this created a safe space for them. Both our hearts were softening and being seen—and we all need to be seen. Their soul became soothed, and as they began to acknowledge their newfound feeling of safety, they would voluntarily say, "Thanks for letting me be here." I appreciated the gratitude; it was healing for both of our hearts.

Gracious words are a honeycomb, sweet to the soul and healing to the bones.
—Proverbs 16:24

Indeed, during their time staying with other friends and family, it was common that they were told, "Get out of my home. You don't belong here." This left feelings of marginalization, devaluation, and anger. Hence, having a space of their own—no matter how small—made all the difference, and suddenly, they now felt seen and heard.

The pandemic was (and to date continues to be) a horrific world event—and yet for some, it brought unexpected blessings due to their newfound time together. This was indeed the case for my loved one, who was able to regroup to some degree. Of course, the consequences of some past behaviors still had to be addressed, and there were occasional setbacks, but generally speaking, they managed to get up each morning and start afresh.

Be gentle with yourself when there are setbacks. As you grow, the circumstances surrounding you will also change to reflect the person you've grown into. This process is not instantaneous; it's a journey.

Perhaps you have a loved one out there in the world who is struggling, too. Many people have loved ones who are struggling today with homelessness, drugs, or alcohol, and many don't know how to embrace these hurting loved ones; they don't understand the depth of what their loved one has gone through. However, love is truly what they need: they need to be seen and heard, especially during their pain. There are great resources out there (*free* resources) to get the help you and your loved ones need. Don't let shame prevent you from seeking help. There's AA (Alcoholics Anonymous) for those battling alcohol addiction; there's Narcotic Anonymous for those with drug addictions; and for the friends and family of those with addictions, there's Al-Anon. That's right, a support group for family and friends of those with addictions! These are support groups with others who are struggling with these same issues that you're facing. You're not alone! For mental health support for the family and friends of those with mental health issues, look for support groups through NAMI (National Alliance on Mental Illness). Often, mental health and substance abuse go together, as the substances get used to alleviate the pain, so you may benefit through both organizations.

There is hope. You can live a life of peace, let go of the drama, and start seeking support from those who understand. You have to be aware, acknowledge your pain, and take responsibility for yourself and step out in action! Remember, we heal in safe relationships—even if these relationships are those formed through support groups. That's the path of growth. It's not easy, but it's worth it!

> *Come to me, all you who are weary and burdened, and I will give you rest.*[29]
> *Take my yoke upon you and learn from me, for I am gentle and humble in heart, and you will find rest for your souls.*[30] *For my yoke is easy and my burden is light.*
> —Mathew 11:28-30

Jesus and God loved us first, just as we are—the sinners, haters, and condemning people that we can be. As humans, we condemned Jesus on the cross. His response before dying, as noted in Luke 23:34, was, "Forgive them, Father, for they know not what they do."

Notably, there is a difference between 1) loving someone and holding them accountable, 2) enabling their addictions and bad behavior, and 3) flat-out denying them love until they are "fixed". It is healthy to say, "Take responsibility for your actions and seek help. I will meet you on your journey. I will not enable your addictions and hurtful behavior. I will not allow you to hurt me or others." Thankfully, Jesus modeled various approaches to helping and healing others; our job is to adjust our method of healing to the personal needs of different people. As authentic disciples of Christ, the Holy Spirit will guide us. Ask Him and then take action!

CHAPTER 14:
RESTORE WHOLENESS AND
LEAD WITH PURPOSE

I KNOW MY PURPOSE: IT is to bring awareness to generational and systemic issues and to be a guide to help awaken people to the administrative Truth of God and the choices they have to change their lives. It's to give preeminence to Jesus Christ in all areas of my life.

I have the heart to teach those who are ready to embrace growth, and the avenue in which I feel called to do this is helping women in leadership, business owners, and executives with their personal and professional growth and to help them lead others and grow their business.

The workplace is the largest mission field on Earth, and we need to develop Christian leaders to be authentic disciples of Christ and help them to grow the people who work for them, integrating their faith with their business so they can focus on people-centric, values-based, compassionate servant leadership. Even those in government can align with servant leadership, as they are (or need to be) community servants!

Leading with love has a huge impact on the business world, with its ripple effects touching all the spheres of influence. Think about this: If you are a business owner or an executive with a team and you grow, you impact the lives of those working close to you. Further, if you develop those around you and nurture all your staff, you begin to change individuals' lives across the company—and as each one of them grows, they impact their families, communities, and government agencies, and your business grows! Ultimately, as each person grows, they each have positive ripple effects that have the potential to spread around the world.

So, do you know your purpose while here on Earth? We each have our own purpose and a unique circle of people in our lives who we're able to influence. Life is like a big jigsaw puzzle: each of us has our portion of the picture, and when we each know our role and perform accordingly, the picture is richer and fuller, with more colors and depth. Without each of us, there are gaps!

Should you not know your purpose and are wondering how you can discover yours: first, identify your strengths—the things that are easy for you, that you do well, and that you enjoy doing. This is harder than it sounds: often, because our strengths come easily to us, we don't think of them as strengths; rather, we tend to dismiss them, thinking anyone can do those things. I have created *The You Factor: Your Gift Mix Workbook* to help you find your gift mix—the special combination of your strengths, talents, education, and life experiences that makes you unique. This guide is invaluable when it comes to establishing your purpose in life. Should you be interested om and truly dedicated to your transformational journey, you can obtain your copy at https://giftmix.candacemae.com.

Remember, the gifts and strengths we have are gifts that were given to us by God. Our gifts are not something we are to take credit for. Remember that your gifts are greater than you: they are from God and are meant to help you serve mankind here on Earth. If you choose to let God work through you, He will use both your strengths and His gifts so you can help other people. It's such an honor to serve humankind by allowing Christ's Spirit to flow in, with, and through you!

Indeed, there are people out there who think that their gifts and strengths are simply who they are and take full credit for them. These people become superior in attitude, growing to be conceited, narcissistic, and controlling. Don't be that person: be humble; be grateful; be kind; be generous; be loving. You will find peace and joy in serving others with the gifts God has granted you.

Also seek to understand your values and how you will work to ensure these values manifest in your daily life. This is critical for you to live an authentic life and to find people with similar values to you to surround yourself with.

To do this, first take inventory of your life: think about what brings you joy and be sure that you are living out those things daily or weekly. This is easier said than done: as I've stated several times already, many of us let life's demands drive our daily lives, mindlessly checking off the list of things to do each day. This leads to us neglecting what we actually value most.

It's good to take inventory of what you value frequently and to assess whether your life is reflecting those values. Do you have a personal life growth plan, or are you taking life one day at a time, being shifted from here to there with no end goal in mind? Have you considered intentionally focusing on designing your life to be all you want it to be? Do you realize you have that ability, or are you coasting through life, letting it pull and push you in random directions?

I offer a comprehensive personal life growth plan that is available to you as a reader in which I walk you through such a process. This includes a comprehensive plan with short- and long-term objectives to design your year (and beyond) so you can go forward with the ability to create the life you want so you're actively and deliberately growing into the person of your greatest desires and realizing the potential God seeded in you. It's well-rounded and includes metrics for measuring your desires and growth. If you'd like to learn more about this, reach out to me at www.candacemae.com, or schedule an appointment with me to discuss (at www.candacemae.com/schedule-an-appointment).

I hope that in this book, I've challenged you to intentionally grow every day. Indeed, as you grow, you will find that the people around you will either grow with you, or you will outgrow them. That is the price of growth: as you grow and live your authentic, value-based life, you will establish and grow healthy relationships and children, and those who don't facilitate such growth in your life will quite naturally fall away. Remember, children learn what they live. Be gentle with yourself, though: children are individuals, and they will make their own choices as they age. Your children's choices (especially adult children's choices) are not a reflection on you; they are accountable for themselves! Keep your adult children in prayer and trust God to work in their lives.

Growth takes time, intention, and energy. Growth is a journey. I left Michigan in 1982 on my journey to California to become my best self, and yet I still am a work in progress thirty-eight years later. During those years, I've had three beautiful children who were born in the middle of my growth journey. I did the best I could at each moment, and though I strived to be a good mom, I fell short in many areas. Still, I continue to grow, and as a grandmother, I'm more seasoned, though not perfect. So be gentle with yourself! Don't expect perfection from yourself—nor from anyone else, for that matter. We are all perfectly imperfect humans; spiritual beings having a human experience.

It's important to periodically stop, reflect on your life, and observe the progress you've made. Let the growth catch up with you so you can own the new you! Once you're intentional about growth, you will realize that *growth is cumulative*: at first, you may be doing a lot of internal growth without a lot to show on the outside—and then one day, you will suddenly realize how much you've grown and the fact that you are a totally different person. When I think of growth, the story of the Chinese bamboo tree comes to mind:

In the Far East, there is a tree called the Chinese bamboo tree. This remarkable tree is different from most trees in that it doesn't grow in the usual fashion. While most trees grow steadily over a period of years, the Chinese bamboo tree doesn't break through the ground for the first four years.

Then, in the fifth year, an amazing thing happens: the tree begins to grow at an astonishing rate. In fact, in a period of just five weeks, a Chinese bamboo tree can grow to a height of ninety feet.
—Eric Aronson

It's been an honor sharing this journey with you. Should you be sufficiently inspired to get started on your journey, this book's companion guide and *The You Factor: Your Gift Mix* workbook are wonderful tools to get you started. This is a workbook I usually bundle with other services, but is one I decided to gift to you as a reader. Should you feel overwhelmed at any point, please do reach out to me so we can explore other ways in which I may be able to assist you, if needed. I have small groups, online courses, coaching, and consulting and business training, as well as a vast treasure chest of resources to guide and stretch you—both personally and professionally. Remember, to grow your business, you need to grow your people. Our professional life is not to be compartmentalized: we carry everything with us. As we grow and as our team members grow, our businesses grow.

I will continue to grow my entire life because growth is important to me and I make it a priority. I encourage you to find a life partner and friends who share your values and embrace their own growth. We are greatly influenced by those around us. The beliefs and programs you pass onto your children will last for generations, and you never know, your children may be the future leaders of our world and society! Give them a strong foundation based on abundant thinking. If you stay stuck in your limiting beliefs and the old patterns you absorbed, you and your children may live a limited life. It takes the same amount of energy to stay stuck as it does to grow; it's just that growth takes deliberate intention and action. Choose wisely!

For me, it's a no-brainer: I choose to grow with intention. I hope you will choose life and growth for yourself, for your staff at work, and for your children—and the generations to come. To be our best selves and the best leaders we can be, we must restore wholeness—and having a relationship with Christ and His Spirit will certainly restore wholeness for better leadership!

ACKNOWLEDGMENTS

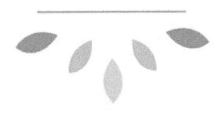

This book would not be possible without the help and support of:

Hayley Paige, owner of Onyx Publishing, and Elise Webb and the entire editorial department.

Kacie Marie Gresch, for being my initial proofreader.

Jacklyn Barcena, for being my marketing/virtual assistant.

Rachael Jayne and Datta Grover, for hosting the writing retreat where this book was born in May 2020.

My thanks also go to all the people who have touched my life to date—for the better, worse, or indifferently—as it is because of my journey and my encounters and experiences with each person whose life has touched mine that I am who I am today.

I am grateful for my identity in Christ, without whom I have no idea how I would have made it through this life!

And my greatest gratitude goes to Jesus Christ's Holy Spirit, who flowed through me to write this book, which was *originally written to me*. I was told to write this book and share it with the masses, so, with obedience, this is what I've set out to do: to share my stories, the lessons I've gleaned and learned along the way, and the scriptures that were provided to me throughout the writing process.

> *So shall My word be that goes forth from My mouth;*
> *It shall not return to Me void,*
> *But it shall accomplish what I please,*
> *And it shall prosper in the thing for which I sent it.*
> —Isaiah 55:11 NKJV

My goal is to share the elixir from my Hero's Journey with those who endeavor to read these pages. May you be deeply blessed and richly inspired.

RESOURCES

The You Factor: Finding Your Gift Mix Workbook (usually bundled with services)
Available to my readers at: https://giftmix.candacemae.com/

Your Companion Guide to *Heaven Within*
Available to my readers at: https://workbook-hw.candacemae.com/

Three Christian Values That Will Increase Your Profit$
Available to my readers at: https://go.CandaceMae.com

You can also reach out to me across various online platforms, including:

Website: CandaceMae.com
Linktree: https://linktr.ee/candacemae
LinkedIn: https://www.linkedin.com/in/candacemaegruber/

Facebook:
Personal Page: https://www.facebook.com/candace.gruber/
Business Page: https://www.facebook.com/CandaceMaeTraining
Private Group: https://www.facebook.com/groups/transforming
                 atoxicculture
Twitter: https://twitter.com/CandaceMae_com

You may also book a call through my online calendar: https://candacemae.com/schedule-an-appointment.

ADDITIONAL RESOURCE

An additional resource by Candace Mae for finding hope...

Powerhouse Women: Survivor to Thriver—sharing the stories of 10 Female Entrepreneurs from the UK, Canada and USA, all of whom overcame trauma and went on to achieve the extraordinary in both life and business.

All proceeds from book sales are donated to the following charities:

The National Coalition Against Domestic Violence (NCADV) (USA)
Women's Aid (UK)
BC Society of Transition Houses (Canada)